Geoffrey of Monmouth's
LIFE OF
MERLIN

Geoffrey of Monmouth at his writing desk.
(*Detail from the Geoffrey Tapestry at Monmouth Priory.*
Photograph © Martin Russell. Reproduced by permission.)

Geoffrey of Monmouth's
LIFE OF MERLIN

A NEW VERSE TRANSLATION

MARK WALKER

AMBERLEY

BY THE SAME AUTHOR

Annus Horribilis: Latin for Everyday Life

Annus Mirabilis: More Latin for Everyday Life

Britannica Latina: 2,000 Years of British Latin

Amida: A Novel

First published 2011

Amberley Publishing
Cirencester Road, Chalford,
Stroud, Gloucestershire, GL6 8PE

www.amberleybooks.com

British Library Cataloguing in Publication Data.
A catalogue record for this book is available from the British Library.

ISBN 978-1-4456-0178-6

Typeset in Palatino nova.
Typesetting and Origination by Amberley Publishing.
Printed in the UK.

CONTENTS

THE LIFE OF MERLIN

INTRODUCTION

The *Life of Merlin* is a strange, fascinating and ultimately bewitching work of medieval artistry set in a semi-mythological era of kings, prophets and madmen. Its eponymous hero is one of the most famous characters in all literature, and it is here for the first time that he is brought centre-stage. The poem's author is also the man who coined the name by which we know his creation today: Merlin.

No one did more to forge the legend of Merlin than Geoffrey of Monmouth. Prophets of similar name had existed in native British folklore long before he wrote – indeed, as we shall see below, Geoffrey derived his Latin *Merlinus* from the Welsh *Myrddin* – but it was Geoffrey who fashioned from a variety of disparate sources the single character whose exploits have been continuously told, re-told and elaborated on ever since. In turn, Geoffrey's high reputation throughout the Middle Ages and into our own times has depended in no small part on the enduring appeal of Merlin.

Geoffrey's Merlin is a multifaceted mixture of opposites: he is ancient yet youthful, dignified yet foolish, familiar yet unknowable. Even today this wise, wild, eccentric character remains the paradigm on which our modern conception of a wizard is based. But the Merlin depicted in Geoffrey's poem is not the staff-carrying, pointy-hat-wearing old man of later tradition.

In fact, he doesn't seem much like a wizard at all. This Merlin is at once a king, a lawmaker, and a madman who shuns society; he is an unpredictable mischief-maker, an inspired prophet, and a repository of cutting-edge scientific knowledge. If this Merlin can be said to resemble any modern wizard at all, he is more like the benevolently tricksterish Wizard of Oz than any of his more obvious descendants – Gandalf or Dumbledore, to name but two.

Merlin was the Alpha and Omega of Geoffrey's literary career. Geoffrey first published his *Prophecies of Merlin* (*Prophetiae Merlini*) as a precursor to his larger *History of the Kings of Britain* (*Historia Regum Britanniae*[1]), in which the *Prophecies* take up the whole of Book 7. Then, towards the end of his life, Geoffrey returned to Merlin one more time in the bold and sometimes baffling *Life of Merlin* (*Vita Merlini*).

With his prose *History* Geoffrey had proved that he was a great storyteller, conjuring a fabulous account of British history worthy of any novelist. But in the *Life of Merlin* he went even further, creating an entirely new genre. The *Life* is quite unprecedented for its time: an epic Latin poem whose subject matter is not only peculiarly British, but also personal and largely domestic in its focus. In Geoffrey's poem there are no Homeric champions contending for supremacy in single combat, nor malicious deities directing the fate of men; the subject is not war or the exploits of a military hero. What Geoffrey gives us instead is something unique: a sustained portrait of one man, his madness and rejection of civil society, his turbulent relationship with friends and family, his strange prophetic gifts, and, in the end, his reinvention as an ideal Renaissance man. The *Life* is a true one-off.[2]

Scholars have long debated Geoffrey's sources, his intentions, and the meaning of his occasionally inscrutable text. But until now there has not been a readily accessible and (more importantly) *readable* translation of the *Life of Merlin* for a general audience. By putting Geoffrey's text into English verse, the aim of the present translation is to provide the non-specialist reader with a version that can be *read* – and enjoyed – not merely studied for its wealth of medieval learning, mythology and history. Though Geoffrey's work will undoubtedly continue to provide fertile material for scholarly debate, it is important not to forget that the *Life of Merlin* is a poem, and it ought to be enjoyed as a poem. If the poetry of this translation brings pleasure to the reader, it will have achieved its aim.

1
GEOFFREY OF MONMOUTH

The few known biographical details of Geoffrey's life can be summarised quickly.[3] Geoffrey was born at the beginning of the twelfth century, *c*. 1100. In his *History of the Kings of Britain* he styles himself *Galfridus Monemutensis*, and at the close of the *Life of Merlin* as *Gaufrido de Monumeta*, so he or his family evidently had some connection with the Welsh border town, though whether he was actually educated at the Benedictine priory in Monmouth, as tradition has it, is not known – nor, indeed, is it entirely clear that he was in fact Welsh, as has been assumed in the past. In some other extant documents Geoffrey's name occurs as *Galfridus Artur*, the relatively unusual name Arthur probably derived from his father – a clue, perhaps, that his family had a long-standing interest in British myth.

He spent much of his adult life at Oxford which, although not yet a university, was already an important centre of learning, and Geoffrey is there styled *magister* ('teacher'), possibly a secular canon associated with St George's College in Oxford Castle. In later life his services were rewarded by ordination as a Bishop and appointment, in 1152, to the new see of St Asaph in North Wales – though it is not certain that he ever took up residence in his bishopric. He died not long after his ordination, in 1155.

While at Oxford Geoffrey wrote the work on which his reputation rests most securely, the *History of the Kings of Britain*, which was in general circulation by about the year 1138. By way of a trailer advertising the longer work, he had already issued the *Prophecies of Merlin* separately in about 1135.

Even for a modern reader, the scope and imaginative breadth of Geoffrey's *History* is breathtaking. By far the largest portion of the narrative is concerned with the battles and exploits of Arthur – and this is the primary reason why the work continues to be read today – including Arthur's final showdown with Mordred at Camlan and the wounded king's subsequent removal to the Isle of Avalon.

But the *History* begins much earlier, with the settling of the British isles by the Trojan exile Brutus (grandson of Aeneas, the hero of Virgil's epic). Thereafter Geoffrey canters through the legendary early kings of Britain, giving us along the way the colourful tale of King Leir and his three daughters (which Geoffrey seems to have invented), until we reach the Romans – whom Geoffrey imaginatively depicts as the barbarian invaders of an ancient and more civilised island nation – and then leads us onwards to the tragic story of Vortigern, who unwisely allies himself with the Germanic brothers Hengist and Horsa, and so precipitates the devastating invasions of the Anglo-Saxons that will ultimately drive the native Britons (i.e. the Celts) to the margins of their own island, the fearsome resistance of war leaders like Arthur notwithstanding.

By the time Geoffrey reaches the events of Vortigern's reign he is able to draw on several earlier sources, especially Gildas (*c.* 500–570), Bede (*c.* 672–735), and the ninth-century *Historia Britonum* of Nennius. But Geoffrey is no mere follower of his predecessors. It is in the context of Vortigern's struggle that Geoffrey departs from these earlier writers to introduce his trump card: Merlin.

2
MERLIN IN GEOFFREY'S HISTORY

In Book 6 of the *History*, Geoffrey relates how the hapless British king Vortigern is betrayed by his erstwhile Saxon allies and forced to surrender much of his kingdom to the marauding invaders. Retreating to Wales he consults his advisors (*magi*), who tell him to build a fortified tower on Mount Snowdon – but the project soon runs into trouble as time and again the king's stonemasons find their foundations swallowed up by the ground. Again the *magi* are consulted, and this time they advise him to kill a young man with no father and pour his blood on the stones. So Vortigern sends envoys throughout what is left of his kingdom to find such a boy, and they soon discover someone whose father is unknown: the young Merlin. It is revealed by the boy's mother, a nun, that a mysterious man had visited her in the convent and made love to her, and that is how she conceived the boy – one of Vortigern's advisors tells the king that this must have been an *incubus*, a part-human, part-angelic spirit (*daemon*). By putting this explanation into the mouth of one of the *magi*, Geoffrey avoids vouching for the truth of the assertion himself, but later writers would expand on his hint to tell how, in fact, Merlin was begotten by a devil.[4]

Boldly, the young Merlin accuses the king's *magi* of being frauds, and then predicts what will be found beneath the site of the king's tower:

> My Lord King [says Merlin], call your workmen and order them to dig up the earth, and you will find a pool beneath it that prevents the tower from standing … Instruct them to drain the pool through channels, and you will see at the bottom two hollow rocks and in those rocks two sleeping dragons.

Amazingly, this is exactly what is discovered, and the king's *magi* – who failed to discern these wonders – are discredited. Suitably impressed, the King and his men gather to hear more of the young man's predictions, so leading us neatly into Book 7, the self-contained *Prophecies of Merlin*.

Geoffrey borrowed the outline of this story from the *Historia Britonum* ('The History of the Britons'), a collection of annalistic records and various other historical narratives compiled around the year 830 and attributed to one Nennius. In the original story, the young man is called Ambrosius and he boasts (rather illogically, given his supposed fatherless state) that his father was a Roman consul. Geoffrey's Merlin claims he is called Ambrosius, too, but Geoffrey distinguishes between this Merlin Ambrosius and the Aurelius Ambrosius, brother of Uther Pendragon, who will (as Merlin prophesies) kill Vortigern, take his crown, and then defeat the Saxon leader Hengest and his son Octa in pitched battles.

Quite what caused Geoffrey to attach the name of an old Welsh prophet called *Myrddin* to the youth in Nennius' Vortigern-Ambrosius tale is not clear, but it was an inspired move. By fusing Ambrosius and Myrddin into Merlin, he created a figure whose prophetic powers could give voice to the nationalistic yearnings of the twelfth-century Welsh under their Norman overlords.[5] The prophecies his Merlin then utter begin with an explanation of the two dragons found sleeping in the hollow stones: one is red, representing the British; the other is white, representing the Saxons. The two will fight, but the red dragon will only prevail when the 'Boar of Cornwall' (Arthur) comes to lead his people. To this day, the red dragon is the symbol of Wales.

Geoffrey's version of Merlin's prophecies, which are 'radically different from the Welsh Myrddin tradition',[6] continue for many pages thereafter. Some refer to events that occurred long before Geoffrey's own century, but the outpouring of prophetic utterances extends into Geoffrey's future, too. Most are deliberately opaque, many clothed in obscure metaphorical language as various beasts – lions, boars, snakes, asses, hedgehogs – are brought in to represent ... well, in the best prophetic tradition, each reader is able to formulate their own interpretation. As a result, each new generation was able to find something applicable to their own times in the prophecies and so they continued to fascinate readers throughout the Middle Ages and beyond (rather like those of Nostradamus would do, and continue to do, up to the present day). As late as the eighteenth century, Merlin was still a byword for political prophecy, thanks to the continuing influence of Geoffrey's picturesque phraseology.[7] But Merlin has more work to do in the *History* than just tell the future.

After Vortigern's death and Aurelius Ambrosius' victory over the Saxons, the new king calls upon Merlin to help him build a monumental memorial to the fallen. The prophet advises that they fetch a stone circle from Ireland, which had been brought from Africa by giants and possessed magical healing properties. Despite his doubts, Ambrosius sends his brother Uther Pendragon with an army to take the stones from the Irish. But after Uther has defeated the Irish king Gillomanius he is unable to find any means of moving the massive stones. Merlin intervenes, laughing – as we shall see,

Merlin's laughter is important in the *Life* – and contrives to move the stones himself, not by magic but with his own *machinationes* ('machines', 'devices'). They are then loaded on to Uther's ships and taken to back to Salisbury plain, where Merlin promptly sets them up again to form the monument we all know as Stonehenge.

As a prophet of future events, Merlin is inspired to speak by 'a spirit', as if some divine agency was speaking through him – just as countless ecstatic prophesyers before him had done, right back to the days of the Pythian priestess of the Delphic Oracle. Uniquely in Geoffrey's narrative, though, Merlin is not just able to see into the future, he is also a master of science (in this case, engineering). He possesses powers that seem magical but are, like those of Mark Twain's Connecticut Yankee, actually the result of knowledge that is unfathomable by those around him. Merlin's lifting of the Irish stones is not *Harry Potter*-style wizardry, rather an example of Arthur C. Clarke's dictum that 'any sufficiently advanced science is indistinguishable from magic'. This scientific side of Merlin's character was still prevalent in the eighteenth century, when Jane Brereton (under the pseudonym 'Melissa') published 'Merlin: A Poem' (1735):

Six Centuries, twice told, are now compleat,

Since *Merlin* liv'd on this terrestrial Seat.

Knowledge appear'd, but dawning to my Sight;

She blaz'd on *Newton* with Meridian Light.

Yet the faint Glimm'rings, which my *Genius* taught,

Beyond the ken, of human Art, were thought.

What I by meer mechanick Pow'rs atchiev'd,

Th' Effects of *Magick* , then, by most believ'd.

To *Stone-henge* , let the Sons of Art, repair,

And View the Wonders, I, erected There.

Try, if their Skill improv'd, Mine, e'er can foil;

Restore the *Giants-Dance* t' *Hibernian* Soil.

Nor in *Geometry* , excell'd alone;

But other *Sciences* to me were known.

I study'd *Nature* , through her various Ways;

And chaunted to this *Harp, prophetick* Lays.[8]

The importance of such knowledge to Merlin will become clearer in the *Life*, as we witness his intimacy with nature and eavesdrop as he and his companion Taliesin discourse on natural philosophy.

Merlin and his 'magical' scientific skill also play an important instrumental role in the conception of the future King Arthur. Geoffrey relates how Uther Pendragon, having succeeded his brother to the throne, becomes infatuated with Igraine (Geoffrey calls her *Ygerna*), wife of the Duke of Cornwall, Gorlois. Uther attacks Cornwall with an army and Gorlois conceals his wife in his castle at Tintagel. Desperate to have his way with her, Uther summons Merlin for assistance. Merlin, moved by the king's evident passion, tells him:

> In order for you to obtain your wish you must make use of methods new and unheard-of in your age. By my medicines I know how to give you the appearance of Gorlois, so that you will seem to be him in every respect. And so if you comply I will make you resemble him ... and you will be able to approach the citadel and Igraine in safety, and to have admittance.

Medicaminibus – 'drugs' or 'medicines' – says Merlin. Is it alchemy or is he, like his distant literary relative Sherlock Holmes, a master of disguise? Either way, he has access to special knowledge unavailable to others, knowledge that is 'new and unheard-of in your age'. Uther takes Merlin's prescribed draught, is transformed (somehow), and is admitted to the castle by the guards who mistake him for their Duke. Then Uther enjoys a night of passion with the compliant Igraine,

> and so on this same night she conceived the most celebrated Arthur, who subsequently deserved by his remarkable virtue to be celebrated.

At this turning point in the narrative Merlin vanishes from the *History* never to return. Surprising though it seems to modern readers, he plays no part in Geoffrey's account of Arthur's reign.[9]

3
THE LIFE OF MERLIN

When we next encounter Merlin in the *Life* he is an old man, though at the beginning of the poem he is also now a king in his own right. After witnessing the death of three (unnamed) brothers in battle, Merlin is driven mad by grief and runs off to the forest to become a 'wild man of the woods' (*siluester homo*). There he laments his misfortunes until a messenger from his sister Ganieda, wife of King Rhydderch, brings him back to Rhydderch's court, where Merlin's wife Gwendoloena is also living. Despite their entreaties, Merlin cannot stand to remain among people and runs back to the forest, only to return at the news of his wife's remarriage, be held captive, then flee again. His sister then builds for him a palatial residence in the forest, where he is at leisure to study the stars and talk science and history with fellow bard Taliesin. After drinking curative spring water he finally recovers from his madness, loses the 'gift' of prophecy and devotes himself to a life of scholarly contemplation.

This portrayal of Merlin did not arise fully formed from Geoffrey's imagination: several events in the *Life* are closely related to legends about other prophetic wild men. But Geoffrey seems to be the only writer of his time who grasped that the similarities between these stories were strong evidence for an original archetype, and the *Life* can be seen as, in part, an attempted literary reconstruction of that archetype. Geoffrey is also at pains to establish with the *Life* that the prophesying wild man of those old tales is one and the same as the Merlin in his *History* who advised Vortigern and his successors.

4
MYRDDIN

The Welsh bard and prophet Myrddin is perhaps the most important inspiration for Geoffrey's work – Geoffrey not only Latinised the Welsh name as *Merlinus*, but for his *Life* adopted at least the outline of the biographical account implicit in the poems traditionally assigned to Myrddin. The earliest surviving texts of these ancient Welsh poems date from the mid-twelfth century (roughly contemporary with Geoffrey himself), but scholars agree that they preserve many poems from a much earlier period.[10] Like Geoffrey's Merlin, Myrddin has the gift of prophecy and wanders mad through the Caledonian Forest. In the poem called 'Sweet Apple-Tree' (*Afallennau*), Myrddin laments:

Sweet apple-tree that grows in the glade!

Their vehemence will conceal it from the lords of Rydderch,

Trodden it is around its base, and men are about it.

Terrible to them were heroic forms.

Gwendydd loves me not, greets me not;

I am hated by the firmest minister of Rydderch;

I have ruined his son and his daughter.

Death takes all away, why does he not visit me?

For after Gwenddoleu no princes honour me;

I am not soothed with diversion, I am not visited by the fair;

Yet in the battle of Ardderyd golden was my torque,

Though I am now despised by her who is of the colour of swans.[11]

The names Rhydderch and Gwenddoleu also occur in the *Life*, as does a battle that resembles (but is not explicitly identified in the poem as) the Battle of Arfderydd, which was fought in about the year 573. And Myrddin's sister Gwendydd becomes the Ganieda of the *Life*. But Geoffrey's narrative is far more substantial than any of the extant Welsh poems – which are not in narrative form anyway – indicating either that Geoffrey had access to a much longer (presumably prose) work that no longer survives, or that he considerably elaborated upon the hints preserved in the poems. The latter seems far more likely: Geoffrey's novelistic skill was more than up to the task of building upon the few biographical hints to be gleaned from the Myrddin poems, and he considerably expands upon the old legends with his sophisticated portrait – uniquely, his Merlin develops from being a traditional 'wild man of the woods' to an erudite visionary who founds an isolated academic retreat for himself and his fellow scholars.

Some commentators have distinguished two different *personae* in Geoffrey's writings: the Merlin-Ambrosius derived from Nennius (*History*) and the Merlin-Caledonius, or 'wild man' Merlin (*Life*) derived from these Welsh poems, arguing that Geoffrey only encountered the Myrddin stories in later life and so was faced with the problem of reconciling his earlier account of Merlin with the madman of Welsh legend. Indeed, even before the twelfth century had passed, Gerald of Wales wrote in his *Itinerarium Kambriae* ('Journey Through Wales', 1191) that:

There were two Merlins: he who was called Ambrosius, since he had two names, and prophesied during the reign of Vortigern, was born of a demon [*incubus*] … the other came from Scotland and was called 'Caledonian', from the Caledonian forest in which he prophesied and 'Silvester', because finding himself in the midst of battle he saw when looking up to the sky a terrible prodigy and becoming mad fled to the woods [*ad siluam siluestrem*] and remained there to the end of his life. This was the Merlin who lived in the time of Arthur, and was said to have prophesied longer and more frequently than the other.[12]

But there is no need to see any contradiction in Geoffrey's work. His Merlin has two different roles to play: in the *History* he is the cunning advisor to kings, actively involved in the events of his times; in the *Life* he is an old man driven insane – two different aspects of one man, two different periods in one life.

5
LAILOKEN

Another of Geoffrey's probable sources is the tale(s) of Lailoken, a wild prophet associated with the sixth-century Scottish Saint Kentigern. In his 1973 scholarly edition of the *Life*, Basil Clarke argued that Kentigern's legendary association with the see of St Asaph (Kentigern, driven from Scotland, was supposed to have founded the Welsh monastery), would have afforded Geoffrey an opportunity to become acquainted with the Lailoken episodes preserved in fragments of an early Kentigern hagiography.[13] Whatever the case, there can be no doubt of the similarities. In one encounter between Kentigern and Lailoken, the mad prophet predicts that he will himself die a threefold death: stoned, impaled on a stake, and drowned at the same time. A variant of this story occurs in the *Life*, when Merlin predicts that a certain youth of Rhydderch's court will also die a threefold death (Chapter 4). Geoffrey cleverly combines this story with another that also occurs in the Kentigern–Lailoken tradition: the infidelity of the queen. Captured by King Meldred, mad Lailoken is heard to laugh when the queen arrives with a leaf caught in her shawl and her husband absently brushes it away with his hand. Asked to explain his laughter, Lailoken eventually reveals:

For a little while earlier, while the queen was committing adultery in the king's garden, the leaf of a tree fell on her head, to betray her and make her adultery known to the king. And this leaf, caught up in her shawl, was what the queen honoured by carrying it into the hall in front of everybody. As soon as the king saw this leaf he at once plucked it off, and in plucking it off he broke it into little pieces. This is how the woman bestowed honour on an enemy who was going to give away her treachery, and how the king did an injury to the friend who made it less likely that the crime would escape him.[14]

In the *Life*, Merlin similarly explains to Rhydderch what the queen (Merlin's own sister Ganieda) has been up to:

> This is the reason I laughed, O King, for at one and the same time
> You can be censured and praised for the same act, blamed and applauded
> As you removed just now that leaf, which the Queen in her tresses
> Carried unmindfully here: more faithful are you by this action
> Than she, she who has lain in the bushes and longed for her lover
> To make love with her there; as she lay with her hair in disarray
> That leaf lodged in her locks, which was plucked by your innocent gesture.
>
> (Chapter 3)

Other legendary wild prophets include the Irish *Suibhne* ('Sweeney'), whose exploits, although written down at a later date than Geoffrey's work, seem to refer back to the same traditional source as Myrddin and Lailoken.

6

ĢEOFFREY'S HUMANISM

With few biographical clues to go on, it is hard to state with any certainty why Geoffrey – more than a decade after the *History* – not only decided to revive Merlin, but make him the hero of his new dramatic poem. It does, however, seem reasonable to assume that two elements of his plan for the *Life* were, as we have already seen, to identify his Merlin as *the* prophetic wild man of legend, and to make clear that this is the same man as the Merlin of his *History*. He achieved the former by incorporating stories associated with figures such as Myrddin and Lailoken into his narrative; the latter by incorporating new prophecies that relate to the events of the *History* (Chapter 6), as well as explicitly linking the earlier book's narrative to Merlin (Chapter 10).

But why, then, are so many pages of the *Life* taken up with learned discussions of natural philosophy? These passages have no parallel in any other wild man legend. And why did Geoffrey choose to write the continuation of his prophet's life story not in the prose of his earlier work, but in the form of a classical epic poem?

To answer both questions, some brief consideration must be given to the state of learning in the twelfth century. Though the term 'humanism' is usually applied to scholars of the fourteenth century and after such as Petrarch and Erasmus – scholars who emphasised classical learning and the study of the liberal arts (the *studia humanitas*, or 'humanities', hence the term 'humanism') – the movement had its precursors in the twelfth century, a time when literacy was on the increase and across Europe the institutions we know as universities were beginning to be founded. Students flocked to centres of learning such as Bologna, Paris and Oxford, where scholars like the philosopher Peter Abelard (1079–1142) challenged orthodox thinking, sometimes at the risk of their own careers. Geoffrey was based in Oxford just when it first began to acquire its academic reputation. Here he would not only have been exposed to what few classical texts were currently available, but must also have been attracted by the opening up of knowledge that embodied what is now called the twelfth-century Renaissance.

Geoffrey's *Life of Merlin* displays this new Renaissance thinking in a number of ways. Notably, he writes in hexameters, the poetic metre that more than any other distinguishes the work of the Greeks and Romans, particularly in the fields of narrative and didactic verse, both of which are amply represented in the *Life*. If he had wanted a popular audience, if he had wanted a sequel to his bestselling *Prophecies* and *History*, prose would have been the natural choice. But Geoffrey chose verse – hexameter verse no less. There could be no better demonstration of his humanist credentials than this display of classical erudition.

We should remember that in Geoffrey's day books were not 'published' in the sense we understand it; rather they were circulated in manuscript and sometimes copied. Even in this restricted sense, Geoffrey's poem was clearly not intended for a large audience – indeed, it survives in only one thirteenth-century manuscript, whereas his *History* survives in at least 217 manuscripts from the same period.[15] The *Life of Merlin* was likely written for and circulated among a small circle of friends centred around the poem's dedicatee, Robert de Chesney. In this group Geoffrey felt able to express himself in a form congenial to his fellow humanists, who would be the only people cabable of appreciating his grasp of classical prosody and hence the depth of his scholarship.

The discourses on natural philosophy in the latter half of the poem reveal Geoffrey's humanist programme in action. Much of this factual material is derived from the writings of scholars who compiled encyclopaedias based on the fragments of learning that had survived the fall of the ancient world. Most important of these was the seventh-century Isidore of Seville, whose *Etymologiae* – an epitome of known classical sources – is Geoffrey's primary source. Other possible sources are Geoffrey's near-contemporary humanists Bernardus Silvestris, Adelard of Bath, Guillaume de Conches, the *De imagine mundi* (*c.* 1100 attributed to Honorius Inclusus) and the *Liber Floridus* of Lambert of Saint Omer.[16]

There are three major discourses: on fish and islands (Chapter 8); springs and lakes (Chapter 10); and birds (Chapter 11) – all of which might be placed under the general heading 'Wonders of Nature'. These factual descriptions of such wonders serve to anchor Merlin's supernatural abilities in a real world context – what seems miraculous on its own is really part of God's grand scheme, as shown by these other 'miracles' of the natural world. For a twelfth-century audience the discourses contained fresh and interesting information about otherwise inexplicable natural phenomena, information moreover derived (apparently) from actual observation rather than Scripture – which was all too often the only written source available. By embedding this material in his poem Geoffrey not only places Merlin firmly inside rather than outside of nature, but also discovered a novel method of edifying his audience. The *Life*, then, can be seen as in part a didactic poem in the classical tradition of Hesiod or Lucretius; these passages are a key part of the poem's scheme and not digressions.

7
MERLIN'S CHARACTER

Most fascinating of all, the central character of Merlin embodies the new Renaissance humanism and its quest for knowledge about the world (what today we would call empirical science, as opposed to the metaphysical speculation often associated with medieval scholasticism). Unlike the traditional bardic version of the earlier tales, Geoffrey's Merlin is very much a 'new man', more suited to the intellectual climate of the twelfth than the sixth century – he is romantically sensitive enough to be moved to madness by the death of his companions; he has an expert knowledge of the natural sciences, including astronomy and astrology (not two distinct disciplines in those days); and he strives to acquire new knowledge, hence his summoning of the bard Taliesin to his forest retreat, which is itself a model community of scholars: cut off from the world, a place purpose-built for study, contemplation and discourse with like minds. Merlin's affection for academic retirement was surely congenial to the scholarly Geoffrey – in this respect at least, Merlin is Geoffrey's *alter ego*.

Even Merlin's prophetic powers are less the product of a medieval mindset predisposed to the miraculous, and more the result of the sage's profound learning. As has already been noted, implicit in Geoffrey's treatment of Merlin's gift and its setting in the context of other miracles of nature is the idea that such wondrous foresight is explicable in natural terms – knowledge is the key to unlocking the secrets of the universe. As Merlin confesses in Chapter 10, his madness gave him access to these 'secrets' – that is, facts of an empirical nature – and with this abnormally heightened understanding of God's design for the world came the ability to make prophecies. For if the world and everything in it is indeed ordained by God (as Geoffrey and all his contemporaries believed), then by a careful study of nature it should in principle be possible to discover God's plan. And this is precisely what Merlin, his senses magnified by madness, seems able to do. Both when Merlin realises that his wife is to remarry (Chapter 5), and when he begins his lengthy prophecy of future events (Chapter 6), he is seen to be studying the movements of the stars and planets. His discovery of Ganieda's adultery (Chapter 3) is more like a Sherlock Holmesian deduction than a miracle. And even when he predicts the young man's threefold death (Chapter 4) and laughs rather cruelly at the fate of various people in the marketplace (Chapter 5), his prophetic powers are not entirely inexplicable; rather they seem to be a consequence of his extraordinary sensitivity to the hidden mechanics of the universe. When Merlin is at last cured of his madness by drinking the waters of a spring, this preternatural sensitivity deserts him, much to his relief: there is, it seems, such a thing as *too much* knowledge.

Mad though he is at the beginning, like his predecessors Myrddin and Lailoken, by the end Geoffrey's Merlin has moved far beyond any of the older archetypes, becoming a kind of Celtic Socrates – an idealised wise man who is both knowledgeable and hungry for more knowledge. Nowhere is Geoffrey's originality more impressive than in the transformation of the traditional wild man of the bardic tales into a thoroughly modern intellectual. But in the process of making him sane, Geoffrey also stripped away much of the mystery that had made the prophetic magician of his *History* so compelling. Almost certainly, I feel, this was his intention – to use the *Life* both to explain and explain away Merlin's 'magic'. But it will come as no surprise to discover that this rational, humanistic portrait of Merlin not only has no precedent, it was not followed by later writers either, all of whom preferred their Merlin to resemble the mad prophet of the beginning, not the sane and scholarly character Geoffrey presents at the end of his poem. Merlin the Magician makes far better copy than Professor Merlin.

8

ABOUT THIS TRANSLATION

Geoffrey's poem is a single continuous narrative, but I have chosen to divide this translation into chapters – partly for ease of reading, but mostly in order to obviate the need for distracting footnotes. This is not a scholarly edition, and I have sought to make the pleasure of reading my priority; so each chapter is prefaced by a brief introduction that summarises the story and explains any potentially obscure references. These explanations are indebted to the two scholars whose editions of Geoffrey's Latin text I have always had at my elbow: John Jay Parry and Basil Clarke (see the Bibliography on page 41). It hardly needs to be added that my verse translation is far less literal then their prose versions.

My translation is written in the same metrical form as Geoffrey's original: the hexameter. The hexameter was the standard metre of ancient epic poetry in both Greek and Latin. It appears in its original Greek form in Homer's *Iliad* and *Odyssey*, and was later adopted by Virgil and the other Roman poets for their own Latin epics. Hardly surprising, then, that this is the metre chosen by Geoffrey to tell his tale of Merlin: he understood the appropriateness of the hexameter as the proper vehicle for narrative verse.

The Latin hexameter line is often referred to as the *dactylic* hexameter, since it consists of six metrical 'feet', each of which is a *dactyl* or, for variation, a *spondee*. A dactyl is a single unit of verse consisting of one so-called 'heavy' syllable followed by two 'light' syllables (see below), making the pattern 'dum-diddy'. A spondee substitutes the 'diddy' for another 'dum', i.e. 'dum-dum'. Or, to express the same thing in musical terms, each metrical 'foot' can be thought of as equivalent to a single bar of music: so, in the case of the hexameter, each bar consists of a crotchet (whole note) followed by two quavers (half notes), with the time signature being 2/4 (march time). And just as with a musical march, the hexameter verse rhythm puts the primary stress on the first beat of each bar. The fifth foot generally remains as a dactyl and the sixth and final foot is almost always a spondee, creating a characteristic cadence at the end of every line: 'dum-diddy dum-dum', as in the English phrase, 'Shave and a haircut'. This repeated rhythmic ending does the same job as rhyme in modern verse: it provides an audible signal that we have reached the end of each line.

But all this is a little misleading, since there is a fundamental difference between classical Latin and English verse: that is, the metrical scheme of the Latin line is not based on word-stress but rather on something called syllable quantity. Latin poets took the principles of quantitative poetry from the Greeks, who had developed a highly sophisticated system of alternating syllables, which are regarded as either 'heavy' or 'light'. It is this pattern of heavy and light syllables that defines the metrical scheme in a line of quantitative verse. This concept of syllable quantity is related to but is not the same as word-stress. Indeed, much Latin verse deliberately sets out to create a tension between the natural stress of the words and the underlying metrical rhythm of the syllables. So, for example, the famous opening line of Virgil's *Aeneid*:

34

Arma virumque canō, Trōiae quī prīmus ab ōrīs

I sing of arms and the man, who first from the shores of Troy ...

(Virgil, Aeneid I.1)

Consists of six distinct feet thus:

1	2	3	4	5	6

Arma vir- |*um*que ca- |*nō, Trōi-* |*ae quī* |*prīmus ab* |*ōrīs*

Where the natural word-stress (in this instance, the first syllable) of the words *cano* and *Troiae* in the middle of the line are 'offset' – or, to use a musical term, syncopated – falling on the second beat of each foot rather than the first (Virgil similarly offsets the monosyllable *qui* in the fourth foot). Such syncopation is difficult to achieve in English verse, where the rhythm is dependent on word-stress. This is not to say that English poets are always forced to place stressed syllables 'on the beat' so to speak – they, too, can indulge in deliberate syncopation – but just that there is a much closer relationship in English verse between metre and word-stress than in its Latin forebear. The greater importance of word-stress in English makes translation of quantitative verse quite a challenge, especially when it comes to the hexameter.

Some classical verse forms are harder to render into English than others. Partly because Latin tends not to use definite and indefinite articles ('the', 'a/an'), and partly because it is an inflected language that eschews our little particle words ('of', 'by', 'with', 'from', etc.), it naturally prefers a trochaic beat (e.g. *Dies irae, dies illa* = '**dum**-di **dum**-di'), whereas English, with its reliance on articles and other connecting particles, falls more comfortably into an iambic pattern. Hence the natural English equivalent of the Latin hexameter has an entirely different beat – the iambic pentameter so beloved of Shakespeare:

<pre>
1   2   3   4   5
A *horse* | a *horse* | my *king-* | dom *for* | a *horse*
</pre>

(Richard III, Act V Scene IV)

Here the use of unstressed pronouns and articles 'push' the primary stress onto the second word of each foot. The Latin hexameter, by contrast, puts its primary stress on the first beat of each foot, something that seems a little foreign to English. As a consequence of this difference in emphasis, many poets have decided not to employ this metre for their English translations. Tennyson famously wrote elegiac lines in *On Translations of Homer*:

> These lame hexameters the strong-winged music of Homer!
>> No – but a most burlesque barbarous experiment.
> When was a harsher sound ever heard, ye Muses, in England?
>> When did a frog coarser croak upon our Helicon?
> Hexameters no worse than daring Germany gave us,
>> Barbarous experiment, barbarous hexameters!

But not all poets agreed. Henry Wadsworth Longfellow produced an English epic entirely in hexameters, *Evangeline* (published in 1847), which eloquently demonstrates that the hexameter can work in English:

> This is the forest primeval. The murmuring pines and the hemlocks,
>> Bearded with moss, and in garments green, indistinct in the twilight.

(Evangeline, 1–2)

The first line of which we can break down into six feet thus:

1	2	3	4	5

This is the | **for**est prim- | **eval**. The | **murm**uring | **pines** and the |

6

hem-locks,

Notice how the primary stress-accent falls on the first syllable of each foot, creating that 'dum-diddy, dum-diddy, dum' effect. So, for example, line 50 of the *Life of Merlin*:

1	2	3	4	5

Still he did | **mourn** for his | **loss** while the | **ter**rible | **slaugh**ter con- |

6

-tin-ued

But in order to avoid monotony, each 'dum-diddy' foot can become a two-beat 'dum-dum' instead. So, line 65:

1	2	3	4	5

Three whole | **days had** | **passed**, while he | **marked time** | **weep**ing and |

6

wail-ing

The first stressed syllable of every line is always the opening syllable. Typically, each line ends with that characteristic 'shave and a hair-cut' cadence. But because few English words, aside from hyphenated compounds such as 'hair-cut', actually end in two stressed syllables I have followed the example of the Latin poets and treated the final syllable of each line as a 'heavy' stressed syllable even when it is not. So when a line ends on a two-syllable word, the final syllable is always metrically 'heavy', though not pronounced as such. I also allow two separate words to close the line, which helps to prevent the monotony of ending every line with a disyllable.

All of which makes for something ever-so-slightly odd, something ever-so-slightly unnatural about these English hexameters. To translate the *Life of Merlin* in iambic blank verse would perhaps have produced a smoother, more idiomatic version; to use English hexameters is perhaps the more eccentric choice. But everything about Geoffrey's poem is eccentric, mysterious, slightly off-kilter. The very oddness of the English hexameter seems to me to be the ideal vehicle for bringing Geoffrey's strange and fascinating narrative to life.

NOTES

1. Geoffrey's history is usually called *Historia Regum Britanniae*, though it should more properly be called *De Gestis Britonum* ('On the Deeds of the Britons'): see the Introduction to Reeve & Wright (2007).
2. 'The *Vita Merlini* is a remarkable work. Geoffrey has created setting, characters, and plot almost *de novo*, an unusual achievement for a medieval writer', Rigg (1992), p. 46. 'The whole poem is written solely for the delight of the reader. This is its virtue; it is a collection of tales, not too carefully composed, but presenting matter which is a blessed change from imitations of classical tales or outworn moralizings', Raby (1934), p. 138.
3. For a longer account of Geoffrey's life, see Curley (1994).
4. A similar motif of a fatherless child also appears in George Lucas' *Star Wars* saga, where it is revealed that, just like his ancient predecessor Merlin, young Anakin Skywalker – Jedi Knight and future Dark Lord of the Sith – was born without a father. Given the many Arthurian motifs in Lucas' space opera, this is unlikely to be a coincidence.
5. Knight (2009), pp. 25–6.
6. Ibid., p. 27.
7. As part of his parody 'Isaac Bickerstaff' predictions Jonathan Swift published *A famous prediction of Merlin, the British wizard*,

written above a thousand years ago, and relating to the year 1709, with explanatory notes, by T. N. Philomath.

8. 'Merlin: A Poem' (1735) by 'Melissa'; the full text is at http://www.sacred-texts.com/neu/arthur/art026.htm

9. Apart from one brief mention at the end of the last book, when it is stated in passing that Merlin had foretold to Arthur the time when God 'no longer wanted the Britons to rule in the island of Britain'.

10. Skene (1868) dates the *Four Ancient Books of Wales* as follows: *The Black Book of Caemarthen* (1154–1189 – i.e. sometime in Henry II's reign); *The Book of Aneurin* (late thirteenth century); *The Book of Taliessin* (early fourteenth century); *The Red Book of Hergest* (fouteenth to fifteenth century).

11. Skene (1868), p. 371.

12. Giraldus Cambrensis (ed. Dimock, 1868), *Itinerarium Kambriae*, Bk. 2 Ch. 8 (p. 133), my translation.

13. Kentigern is also known as St Mungo. His *Life* was written *c.* 1185 by Jocelin, some twenty years after Geoffrey's death, but fragments of an earlier *Life* were discovered in the fifteenth century, and it is these that contain the Lailoken stories.

14. Clarke (1973), p. 233.

15. Curley (1994), p. 111; Reeve & Wright (2007), pp. vii–viii.

16. Curley (1994), p. 118; Clarke (1973), pp. 6–11.

BIBLIOGRAPHY

(1) Geoffrey of Monmouth editions

Clarke, B. (ed., 1973) *Life of Merlin*, University of Wales Press. [Latin text with parallel English translation, notes and introduction]

Parry, J. J. (ed., 1925), *Vita Merlini*, BiblioBazar. ['print on demand' paperback reprint – English translation followed by Latin text]

Reeve, M. D. & Wright, N. (eds., 2007), *The History of the Kings of Britain*, Boydell Press. [Parallel English–Latin text]

(2) Secondary sources

Curley, M. J. (1994), *Geoffrey of Monmouth*, Twayne Publishers.

Knight, S. (2009), *Merlin: Knowledge and Power Through the Ages*, Cornell University Press.

Raby, F. J. E. (1934), *A History of Secular Latin Poetry in the Middle Ages*, Vol. 2, Clarendon Press.

Rigg, A. G. (1992), *A History of Anglo-Latin Literature 1066–1422*, Cambridge University Press.

Skene, W. F. (1868), *The Four Ancient Books of Wales*, Vol. 1, Edmonston and Douglas.

Tolstoy, N. (1985), *The Quest for Merlin*, Hamish Hamilton.

THE LIFE OF MERLIN

Carminis Personae

GANIEDA – Merlin's sister, married to King Rhydderch.

GWENDOLOENA – Merlin's wife.

MAELDIN – A madman.

MERLIN – Prophet, madman, scholar, King of the Demetae, former advisor to British kings.

PEREDUR – Ally of Merlin and Rhydderch, leader of the Venedoti.

RHYDDERCH – King of the Cumbrians, husband of Merlin's sister Ganieda.

RHYDDERCH'S RETAINER – An unnamed servant who sings to Merlin.

TALIESIN – Bard, learned friend of Merlin.

PREFACE

The poem opens with a flattering address to Geoffrey's friend Robert de Chesney, who was Bishop of Lincoln from 1148 to 1166 – his appointment establishes the earliest date for the composition of the poem. Robert seems to have been a popular replacement for the previous incumbent, Alexander, who apparently didn't favour Geoffrey (line 7). The 'bards of the ancients' (line 13) paraphrases a rare direct quotation from classical poetry, specifically Ovid (*Epistula ex Ponto* 4.16). Geoffrey's actual lines are: 'But I lack the skill, were Orpheus and Camerinus and Macer and Marius and Rabirius of the mighty voice to sing through my mouth'. Geoffrey was probably quoting Ovid from memory. A conventional invocation to the Muses of poetry (*Camenae*) follows.

* * *

Merlin, his madness, the mischievous muse of the poet prophetic

I am preparing to sing; friend Robert peruse this my poem,

Glory of bishops, correct it now calmly with sensible pen-strokes,

You the receiver of wisdom divine whom Philosophy favoured,

Sprinkling her nectar on you – dear leader and worldly instructor

Smile at my projects and plans, on your poet bestow now a fortune

45

Kinder than once was bestowed by the one you succeeded, deserving

Worthy promotion at last, your repayment for merit and honour:

Priests and the people alike did petition for one who is blameless,

One who is useful to all, good, spotless, of lineage sublime: 10

Whence you arrived and our Lincoln was blessed, to the stars elevated.

Hence my desire to bid welcome in song that is worthy of plaudits,

Though my own skills are unfit for the task were the bards of the ancients

Singing in chorus with me and their muses sang harmonies tuneful.

Sisters of poetry, sing I implore, join voices together,

As is your wont, let us sing we our theme as we pluck on the harp-strings.

*   *   *

Chapter 1
MERLIN'S MADNESS

Merlin is introduced as a famous prophet but also as the king of the southern Welsh Demetae tribe. Another Welsh king, Peredur of the Venedoti (modern Gwynedd), goes to war against Gwenddoleu, a southern Scottish king. Peredur is accompanied both by Merlin and Rhydderch, king of the Cumbrians – the Welsh term *Cymru*, from which modern Cumbria is derived, originally referred to speakers of the Welsh language, including those who lived in *Y Gogledd*, 'the North'. But Geoffrey's Latin *Rodarcus* is sufficiently far removed from the name Rhydderch to suggest a deliberate distancing of this (literary) character from the historical king of Strathclyde, Rhydderch Hael (d. 614).

What follows is loosely inspired by the Battle of Arfderydd (modern Arthuret in Cumbria), *c.* 573, during which Gwenddoleu was defeated and Lailoken (see the Introduction) was said to have been driven mad. But unlike Merlin, Lailoken seems to have fought on Gwenddoleu's side. Furthermore, Geoffrey is conspicuously vague about the actual site or time of this battle – perhaps a deliberate part of his strategy to fuse the various traditional mad men tales into a single narrative. The death of 'three dear brothers' (presumably those of Peredur, but again Geoffrey is vague) who were Merlin's companions causes him to lament inconsolably. Such is his grief that he becomes mad and runs off to live as a wild man in the Caldeonian Forest, a wooded area stretching over much of southern Scotland – both Myrddin and Lailoken fled in madness to this forest; it is also mentioned as a site of one of King Arthur's battles in Ennius' *Historia Brittonum*.

*   *   *

Now passed numberless years, passed numberless kings in their due course,

Meanwhile Merlin the Briton was hailed by the world as a famous

King and a prophet whose word was as law to the prideful Demetae,

Singing of things yet to come he held sway in the counsels of leaders.   *20*

Then there arose sad strife and division among all the nobles

Leading to battles and war fought fiercely throughout all the kingdoms –

Innocent people, their homes, and their cities destroyed by the conflict.

War by Peredur was brought to the Scots, and his fierce Venedoti

Fought with Gwenddoleu the king of that realm, and a day was appointed,

Troops were assembled, and kings on the field now surveyed their own squadrons:

Both sides matched in their deadly desire were now rushing to slaughter.

Merlin arrived on the field with Peredur as battle was started,

Rhydderch the King of the Cumbrians too – men like in their fierceness,

Both with invidious swords were now slashing at any opponents.   *30*

Three dear brothers attracted by war came to follow their brother,

Killing the foe they unceasing pursued their rebellious rivals,

Such good service they did as they burst through the hostile formations

Until they fell, killed, dead – and the sight was such sorrow for Merlin:

Mourn, O Merlin, and thus through the ranks shall you bellow your sadness:

'Let not importunate Fate be so harmful to me nor so wicked

That it shall snatch from my arms these companions as dear as courageous:

They were the terror of kings without number and provinces far-flung.

Doubt and uncertainty dog men's footsteps and death is their neighbour,

Death the eternal controller of men, who conceals a deadly   40

Weapon to drive out life from the miserable bodies of mortals.

Who will now stand here beside me? Which of you youths in your armour,

Worthy and brave, will now come to my aid and repel the marauding

Chiefs and their onrushing troops, men busily plotting my downfall?

Bold youths, your own boldness compels you to sacrifice youthful

Beauty and beautiful years of your youth: as you charged the formations

Just now, armed for the fight, you destroyed all those standing against you:

But now you strike at the ground with your red blood bloodily sprinkled.'

So did he pour out his tears, tears wasteful and useless in battle,

Still he did mourn for his loss while the terrible slaughter continued: 50

Troops clashed, rushing together the enemies felled one another,

Blood flowed freely and everywhere men died, many on each side.

At last, summoning troops from the field now the Britons have gathered,

Standing together they charge, and together they fall on the Scotsmen,

Dealing out wounds on all sides they destroy all opposing their onslaught,

Nor do they cease nor rest but when, turning their backs and retreating,

Foes flee – scattering enemies fleeing through devious pathways.

Merlin then summoned his friends from the battle, implored them to bury

Those three brothers so dear in a chapel of fine decoration.

Mourning in grief for the men now his tears fall in rivers unending,   60

Hair he besprinkles with dust, and his clothes he now rips from his body

Falling to sprawl on the ground, now around and around he goes whirling:

Friendly Peredur consoles him, dukes and his noblemen likewise.

Nothing avails, inconsolable he can't bear their entreaties.

Three whole days had passed, while he marked time weeping and wailing,

Food he refused, so great was the grief that inflamed his deep sorrow;

Then a new madness arose and retreating a thief in the night-time

Such were his moans that he filled up the skies as he speedily withdrew

Into the forest and hid, yet concealed his flight from observers.

Groves he delighted to enter and lurked glad underneath ash-trees,   70

Marvelled the man at the animals grazing in glades that were grass-filled,

Follows them now, now runs with a swift stride, running surpasses.

Roots of the plants he consumes, he consumes plants, eating with gusto

Fruits from the trees and the sweet black berries on burgeoning brambles:

Wild is he now, a true man of the woods as to trees dedicated.

Summer he passed in this way, all summer discovered by no-one,

Family, friends too now he forgot and his name he abandoned,

Hiding amid the arboreal groves he was clothed like a wild thing.

But see: winter is stealing away all the nourishing grasses,

Fruits too, food from the trees are all gone and it leaves him with nothing.   80

Now he complains of his misery, cries in a voice to be pitied:

'O Christ, God of the heavens advise me: where shall I linger?

Where on the earth shall I go now I'm starving and food is depleted?

Nor can I see any grass on the ground nor fruits on the branches:

Seven and twelve were the trees that once bore me the sweetest of apples,

Here they once stood but are gone now – suddenly stolen by someone,

Suddenly fallen, but where? Here, here do they stand, I can see now:

Thanks be to Fortune who gives with one hand and yet takes with the other,

Gone are the apples and fruits, gone too are the rest of the foodstuffs,

Gone are the leaves from the trees, I am punished by Fate without mercy,   90

Since I cannot wear leaves for my clothes nor partake of the fresh fruits:

Both are consumed by the rains of the winter and blustering South wind.

If deep under the ground by chance I find turnips there growing,

Greedily pigs come a-running and boars too, snapping with voracious

Jaws they then steal my food, food dug from the earth by my labours.

Dear wolf, you are my guide through the woods and you follow my footsteps,

Walking together we wander the groves; yet you scarcely can stagger

Past fields: hunger so harsh has condemned us both to be feeble.

You came before me to live in these woods, and before me did old age

On you bestow white hairs. Is it true that your mouth is still empty,   100

You do not know where to find food? Are there not beasts in abundance,

Goats and such creatures to seize in your jaws? I assume you are able:

Or has detestable old age stolen your strength for the pursuit?

All that remains is to fill up the air with your ravenous howling:

Weary you lie stretched out on the ground and your limbs are unmoving.'

*   *   *

Chapter 2
THE WILD MAN OF THE WOODS

After enduring the deprivations of winter, Merlin is at last discovered by a retainer sent to look for him by his sister, Ganieda, wife of Rhydderch. The retainer sings to Merlin of his wife's and his sister's grief – mention of the three heroines from classical mythology (lines 178–9) who had also been abandoned by their lovers shows that Geoffrey knew at least part of the *Heroides* of Ovid, in which the women tell their own tales: Queen Dido of Carthage was abandoned by Aeneas; Demophoon, son of Theseus, marries Phyllis but leaves her; while Achilles loved Briseis in *The Iliad*, but was forced to give her up to Agammemnon. Thanks to the persuasive power of the retainer and his song, Merlin is brought back to his senses and agrees to return to Rhydderch's court.

*   *   *

So he proclaimed while he wandered through groves and dense thickets of hazel:

Words that were heard by a man who was passing, which halted his progress.

Now he directed his path to the place where the speaker declaiming

Cried out: found he the place, and so found there the man who had spoken.

Merlin espied him and fled, as the traveller running to pursue   *110*

Tried to detain him but failed: swift Merlin retreated too quickly.

Back turns the traveller, back to his path and the road where he started,

Moved by the plight of the fugitive man he returns to his journey.

Suddenly here on the road comes another, a man from the royal

Cumbrian court, King Rhydderch his master, the happiest husband

Blessed in his marriage to sweet Ganieda the sister of Merlin:

She who lamenting his plight sent forth to the forests and remote

Regions retainers to search for her brother and summon him homewards;

One of her men met the traveller, meeting they fell now to talking,

He who was seeking for Merlin then sought news, questioned the other   120

Whether in forests or glades he had seen such a man as this Merlin?

'Indeed so: there in the depths of the dark Caledonian Forest,'

Came the reply, 'a man like that who then fled at my approach,

Swiftly he fled through the oaks, and so doing denied me a meeting.'

Hearing these words the retainer departed to search through the valleys

And through the dense woodlands, and the loftiest peaks of the mountains

He passed by and in secret locations he sought and kept searching.

There was a fountain on top of a tall and precipitous summit,

Girdled by hazels on all sides, thickly surrounded by thickets:

There sat Merlin alone, there watched he the whole of the woodland,   130

Watched all the animals' joy in their sport and delight in their frolics.

To here silently climbed the retainer with tentative footsteps

Seeking the man: here, finally, saw both the fountain and Merlin

Sitting beside, who lamented his lot with these tokens of hardship:

'Ruler of all things, what is the reason and why does it happen

That four times in a year come the seasons and each is distinctive?

Spring by its own will brings forth flowers and fronds in abundance,

Summer produces the fruit, and the autumn then ripens the produce;

Winter then follows with ice to devour all things in its cruelty,

Bringing the rain and the snow to divide and the storms to do damage;   140

Nor can the soil grow radiant flowers of various colours,

Nor can the oak grow acorns, or fruit trees redden their apples.

Would that the winter was not, and that white hoar-frost was thus banished,

Let it be spring, let summer return with the song of the Cuckoo,

Sacred the song of the Nightingale: let it thus soften my grieving

Heart, as the chaste Dove cleaves to its partner in token of wedlock,

While in the new leaves birds with their voices harmonious upraised

Sing, and by singing the birds warm me with melodious fervour;

Fresh from the earth comes the odour of fresh spring flowers now blooming;

Fountains arise from the green grass, springs that are murmuring sweetly   150

Mingling their voice with the white Dove under the branches here warbling

Soft tunes, bringers of sleep and of slumber to soothe now my troubles.'

So the retainer did hear the complaints of the prophet and artless

Did forestall repetition with tunes on the lyre which he carried

Thus to beguile and caress mad fury and soften such anger,

And with his fingers exciting laments struck strings in succession,

Skulking behind he then sung to the bard with expression unbridled:

'Dire are the groans and the moans Gwendoloena the wife of the prophet

Pours forth: weeping in grief, Gwendoloena adds tears to her sorrow;

Pitiful tears of the fair Gwendoloena have moved me to pity.   160

In all Wales there are none who surpass her in grace and in beauty,

Even the goddesses pale in comparison – leaves from the Privet,

Roses that bloom in the spring, and the fragrance of fields full of Lilies

Likewise: only in her is the glory of radiant springtime;

Twinkling like stars in the night twin eyes blaze, light up the heavens,

Shining in splendour her hair glows golden and gold is its lustre.

All this has perished and died, all grace, all beauty has perished,

So do her cheeks turn pale, and her snowy complexion is faded,

Wasting her days with lamenting, no longer the woman she once was.

Where is her husband? she asks. Is the life he once led now extinguished?

Has Death snatched him away? Not to know is a torment and torture,   170

Miserably pining she melts in the tears that her grieving produces.

Grieving together with fair Ganieda, who mourns for her brother

Lost in the woods: both cry and lament and can never be consoled:

One for her brother now weeps while the other is mourning a husband,

Weeping together they waste all their time and their energy grieving,

Roving by night through the sheltering groves they are weary and restless,

Not sleep, not food brings them refreshment so great is their sadness:

Just as Sidonian Dido did grieve when her lover departed,

And as poor Phyllis lamented her lost love, Briseis also,

So mourn sister and wife, and by torments internal are inflamed.'   *180*

Thus the retainer did sing in such serious strains and while singing

Softened the ears of the bard with his tune, so that Merlin might gentler

Weep and together rejoice with the singer who roused him from madness.

Quickly the prophet arose and in mischievous tones to the youthful

Singer he spoke and implored him to pluck at the strings with his fingers

One more time and repeat now his earlier elegies sublime.

So he complied and his fingers again crossed over the courses

Forming anew the refrain as commanded, compelling the madman

Slowly to lay down lunacy, charmed by the magic of music:

Merlin returned to his right mind, his old self he remembered,   *190*

Madness he loathed and despised, at his folly he felt so astonished

Now that his mind was restored and restored to his mind were his senses.

Pity he felt for the names of his sister and wife and he uttered

Words of remorse as his reason revived, and he asked to be taken

By his new friend to the court of the King, and the other assented:

To King Rhydderch they went therefore, and with forests abandoned

They set out, and rejoicing together arrived at the city.

*   *   *

Chapter 3
MERLIN AT COURT

Merlin's sister Ganieda and her husband welcome his return, but the sight of so many people drives poor Merlin out of his wits again. Despite Rhydderch's best efforts, Merlin desires only to return to solitude in the forest. The Wayland of lines 217-8 (Geoffrey's Latin is *Guielandus*) probably refers to the legendary Wayland the Smith who forged a mail shirt for Beowulf and is mentioned in Kipling's *Puck of Pook's Hill* as a mythical sword-maker. Geoffrey places him at *Urbs Sigenus*, a name probably transferred to the Welsh town of Caernafon from the nearby Roman fort of Segontium. Rhydderch eventually resorts to physical restraint to prevent his friend from fleeing back to the woods, but in an incident that also occurs in the Lailoken fragments (see the Introduction) Merlin just laughs when he sees that the king is being cuckolded by his wife.

*   *   *

So now the Queen did rejoice at her brother returned from the forest,

So did his wife celebrate his arrival, rejoiced in her husband:

Doubling their kisses they vied one another with arms now encircling   *200*

His neck, so much moved by affection were both of his ladies.

Likewise Rhydderch the King did receive him with suitable honour,

And all the men of the court did proclaim his return through the city.

But when Merlin then saw this crowd of importunate mankind

Pressing around, he could not stand it nor bear their entreaties:

Madness returned and his mind fell under the spell of delusion

Once more: back to the woods like a thief he was furtively fleeing.

Rhydderch then ordered his friend to be held and a guard was appointed,

And then the King himself with his lyre soothed Merlin's new madness,

Grieving implored his dear friend to rejoice in his reason and linger   210

Here at the court with his friends and his family, shunning the forest

Neither desire thus to live in the wild like a dangerous creature

Nor skulk under the trees when he might wield royal dominion

Instead and, sceptre in hand, give laws to an arrogant people.

Rhydderch then promised to give gifts generous, rich and abundant:

Offered to him clothes, birds, swift horses to tempt his reluctant

Friend, gold too, bright glittering gems, cups wrought by that Wayland

Smith of Caernafon, and each he did offer to Merlin and counselled

That he remain with the King and relinquish the groves and the woodland.

Merlin rejected the gifts, spurned them, to the King he responded: 220

'Nobles who think they are needy should have such delicate morsels,

For moderation means nothing to them, and they revel in excess.

I for my part choose life in the great Caledonian forest,

Longing for broad Oak leaves and the grass-filled emerald meadows

Under the high peaks – such are my pleasures, not courtiers' trifles.

Each to his own, O King: as the lush Caledonian nut-trees

Nourish my soul so I favour the place more than all of your riches.'

Finally Rhydderch now grasped that his gifts were unable to restrain

Sorrowful Merlin the mad, so he bound him with shackles unmoving,

Chains to prevent him from fleeing to wild uninhabited forests.   230

When poor Merlin discerned he was bound and unable to escape

To his beloved Caledonian wood he resumed his lamenting,

Liberty lost he was sad and in sadness determined on silence,

Joy he removed from his face and his features were empty and vacant,

Nor did he utter a word or allow the expression of laughter.

Wishing to see her dear husband the Queen meanwhile was traversing

The court; warmly he greeted his wife, as was fitting, and clasping

Her by the hand he did ask her to sit and embracing her gladly

Pressed to her lips fond kisses from his – and so doing he noticed

Lodged in her tresses a leaf; with his hand he then grasped and abstracted   240

It and then threw it away as he joked with his wife and his darling.

Turning his eyes to the pair, now Merlin gave vent to his laughter,

Laughter that caused all the men who were present to gaze at the prophet,

Wondering why he did laugh who had vowed to refrain from amusement.

Likewise Rhydderch the King was amazed and he questioned the madman

What were the reasons that caused him to laugh and be suddenly mirthful?

Rhydderch augmented his words with a promise of gifts in abundance,

Keeping his counsel the bard still refused to explain his enjoyment:

More were the prizes and more were the prayers that the King then did offer,

Pressing the prophet to speak; and then finally Merlin assented, ²⁵⁰

Since he was hurt by the offer of gifts, to explain his refusal:

'Miserly men love gifts and the greedy for presents do labour,

Bending their will to wherever commanded, complaisant and supine,

Bribes have corrupted their hearts, their possessions no longer sufficient.

Acorns and glistening springs that flow through the odorous meadows

Of Caledonian woods, such treasures for me are sufficient,

I am not moved by your bribes – let the miser delight in your bounty.

Unless you free me now to return to the emerald valleys

I will refuse to supply explanation and cause for my laughter.'

Hence King Rhydderch now knew that his gifts could not sway his opponent₂₆₀

Nor could persuade him to fix on a reason for laughing and smiling,

So therefore he commanded his men to release him from bondage,

Granting him licence to seek for seclusion in wilderness forests,

Such was his wish to discover the cause of the laugh of the prophet.

At last Merlin, rejoicing in freedom, decided to admit:

'This is the reason I laughed, O King, for at one and the same time

You can be censured and praised for the same act, blamed and applauded

As you removed just now that leaf, which the Queen in her tresses

Carried unmindfully here: more faithful are you by this action

Than she, she who has lain in the bushes and longed for her lover ²⁷⁰

To make love with her there; as she lay with her hair in disarray

That leaf lodged in her locks, which was plucked by your innocent gesture.'

News of this crime brought grief to the King who was gripped by a sudden

Sorrow, and turning his gaze from her face he rejected his dear wife,

Damning the day he'd consented to join her in union of wedlock.

She was unmoved by the sad King, hiding her shame with pretended

Laughter she turned to her spouse and addressed to him words of such comfort:

'Why are you sad, my dear? Why angry with me and my actions?

Why do you damn undeserving your wife? Do you credit this madman

Missing his reason, believe his mendacities mingled with half-truths?   *280*

Thus is a man who believes mad things more a fool than the madman.

I am not fooled by his lies; therefore I will prove to you clearly

That his delirium drives out truth and compels him to falsehood.'

*   *   *

Chapter 4
THE THREEFOLD DEATH

In an attempt to refute the madman's accusation of her infidelity, Ganieda tries to trick her brother into predicting three different deaths for one and the same young man. The king is persuaded that Merlin is mistaken, but in a later aside we learn that the youth will indeed die a threefold death (this motif of the triple death occurs in other madman tales, but is usually applied to the mad prophet himself).

Ganieda then summons Merlin's wife Gwendoloena to try and persuade him to stay with them – both the character and her name seem to be Geoffrey's own invention. Merlin responds coldly to the women's entreaties. Five lines following line 339, 'This was the tenor of Merlin's reply …', have been omitted – they are difficult to understand, probably textually corrupt and possibly spurious. For the curious, they translate something like this: 'I don't want, sister, a beast which pours out spring water from its gaping mouth as from the virgin's urn in the summertime, nor will I alter my care like Orpheus long ago when Eurydice gave her baskets to be held by the boys before she swam across the sandy Styx.' Merlin gives his wife permission to remarry in his absence and then hurries back to his beloved forest.

*   *   *

Now in the court was a boy, one youth in the midst of so many:

Once she had noticed this lad, the ingenious Queen fell to scheming

And she devised then a plan to confuse and confound her own brother.

Hence she commanded the boy to be present and begged of her sibling,

'Brother predict now the death of this boy and his manner of dying.'

'Dearest of sisters,' he said, 'as a man he will fall from a cliff-face.'

Laughing at this she then ordered the boy to depart and exchange   290

What he was wearing for new clothes, trimming his hair at the same time,

So when he came back in he would seem to be totally different.

This he obeyed and returned to the court, as commanded, in disguise.

Then once more did the Queen ask, 'Brother reveal to your dearest

Sister by what means this boy must die, how will it happen?'

Merlin replied, 'When he reaches his peak, though his mind be unsettled,

He will succumb to a terrible, violent death in a tree-branch.'

When he had spoken the Queen then addressed these words to her husband:

'Thus was the false soothsayer so able to bring you to folly,

So that you thought I committed a wicked and horrible offence.   300

But if you wish to discover the reason my brother has spoken

Such things, then you will find that he lies and accuses me falsely,

Since all the while he is plotting to flee from this court to the forest.

Heaven forfend, I would never relinquish my chastity, spotless

Your bedchamber will be while a breath still remains in my body;

Merlin was proved to be wrong, once more his mistake will be exposed:

64

You be the judge', said she and then silently ordered the young man

To go away and to dress like a woman then make a new entrance.

Doing as ordered the boy changed clothes and returned as if female,

Waited in front of the bard as the Queen in amusement was asking: 310

'Well, now, brother do tell, if you can, of the death of this maiden.'

'Maiden or not,' he replied, 'she will meet with her death in a river.'

So he predicted, and Rhydderch responded by scornfully laughing

At the mistake: one boy was to die three times in the future!

So did the King now believe that Merlin's assertion was untrue

When he had mentioned his wife, and regretted his anger and contempt:

Seeing her husband's remorse and rejoicing, the Queen came with kisses,

Soothing and flattering him, and by these she restored him to gladness.

Meanwhile, Merlin was plotting escape to the woods and the forests:

Leaving his house, he demanded the gates be unfastened and opened; 320

But Ganieda was blocking his exit and pleaded with wasteful

Tears that he stay with her here, and abandon this madness forever.

Rashly refusing her pleas he resumed his intended departure,

Kept on demanding the gates be unbolted while striving for freedom,

Beating, berating the servants – by beatings compelling assistance –

Until the Queen saw his lust to depart could no longer be fettered.

So she then asked Gwendoloena to come and attend his departure:

As a suppliant she came, and entreated her husband to tarry,

But he rejected her prayers, as he neither was wanting to tarry,

Nor, as his wont once was, to rejoice in the sight of his lady.   330

Grieving she melted in tears and her hair fell torn and dishevelled,

Scoring her cheeks with her nails she collapsed on the ground and lamented.

Moved by her plight then the Queen spoke coldly to Merlin in anger:

'Your dear wife Gwendoloena is mourning for you and for herself.

What will she do – will she marry again or remain as a widow,

What do you want her to do? Will she follow your lead to the forest,

Happily worshipping groves with her husband for company, gladly

Living in meadows of green, with the love of her spouse as her reward?'

This was the tenor of Merlin's reply as he spoke to his sister:

'Spurning you both I am freed from the defect of women's affection.   340

Therefore, give her the right to be wed to a man of her choosing,

Only beware that this man who is hoping to take her in wedlock

Does not seek me out, nor wilfully stand in my presence:

Let him avoid an encounter with me lest by such provocation

He thus compels me to strike with the shimmering blade of my weapon.

Come though the day of the wedding festivities, lawfully given,

When all the various viands are placed in the hands of the feasters,

I will be present among them, bearing a virtuous present,

Which will enrich Gwendoloena the bride on the day of her marriage.'

So he did say as he walked and then bid both women a farewell,   350

Eagerly seeking the woods now, freed from restraining obstructions.

Sad Gwendoloena remained in the doorway watching her husband,

As did the Queen, both moved by the plight of their suffering loved one;

They were amazed that the madman was able to know all their secrets,

But his account of the hidden affair of his sister above all,

Though they assumed he had lied when he spoke of the death of the youngster

And had said there were three when he should have predicted one only.

Over the years this prediction was thought to be false and mistaken,

Until the boy came of age, when it finally came to fruition.

As he was hunting the boy, now a man, with his dogs for companions,   360

Spied in the bushes a hind that was hiding, concealed in some branches;

So he released all his hounds, and they chased the unfortunate creature

Throughout devious pathways, filling the air with their howling;

While he was spurring his horse and pursuing the pack through the byways,

First with his horn then with voice he encouraged his hunting assistants,

Faster and faster he urged them to come and be quick in their coming.

There was a mountain both lofty and broad and encircled by boulders,

And at its bottom a river was flowing across a wide meadow:

There did the beast in its flight flee, passing the mountain and river,

Seeking a place of concealment to hide in the manner of its kind.   370

There did the young man rush, and so over the mountain he hastened,

Taking a straight path, seeking the hind in the rocks and the rubble.

But as his eagerness pushed him to climb and continue to clamber

His mount slipped from a high rock, he, too, fell from the cliff-face,

Purely by chance as he fell from the heights to the depths of the river

His foot caught on a branch as the rest of his body was submerged,

So he was killed by a fall and was drowned and was hanged from a tree-branch:

Hence by this three-fold death was the prophecy finally fulfilled.

*   *   *

Chapter 5
GWENDOLOENA'S WEDDING

When Merlin's astrological skills alert him to the imminent wedding of his wife, he gathers the beasts of the forest and hurries to the nuptials – but things do not go well for the groom. Captured again, Merlin is miserable and is led through the marketplace in the hope of reviving his spirits. But the mad prophet just laughs mysteriously, so Rhydderch promises to release him if he explains his strange behaviour, thus giving Merlin an opportunity to demonstrate his prophetic powers. When it is found he has spoken the truth, Rhydderch is forced to honour his promise. Ganieda pleads with him to remain, but Merlin asks her instead to build for him a house in the forest where he can live during the harsh winter and devote himself to astronomy and other studies.

The Constantinus and Conan of lines 395–6 were legendary kings of sixth-century Britain, mentioned by Gildas whose account Geoffrey adapts in his *History* – Constantine succeeds Arthur when the latter is transported to the Isle of Avalon following the battle of Camlan in 542. After just three years, Constantine is killed by his nephew Conan (Aurelius Conanus). The chronology suggested here doesn't tally with placing Merlin at the Battle of Arfderydd in 573 – Geoffrey may have been well aware of this, and it is one reason he refrained from specifying the name of the earlier battle.

Merlin's surprising appearance riding a horned stag (lines 421–30) recalls the Celtic horned god Cernunnos, according to Nikolai Tolstoy (see the Bibliography), who also argues that Geoffrey misunderstood an earlier source in which Merlin was said to wear an antlered helm, and it was this that he threw at the bridegroom; the Irish wild man Suibhne also possesses dominion over stags. The marketplace incidents of the beggar who is unwittingly rich and the unfortunate youth with his shoes (lines 447–71) may be derived from an Oriental souce.

*   *   *

Merlin had entered the woods and was living a brutish existence,

As he subsisted on ice-cold moss in the harshness of winter   *380*

He was exposed to the rain and the snow and the blasts of the bitter

North wind – hard was his life, but more pleasing to him than dispensing

Laws in the cities or fighting ferociously fierce populations.

Years slipped by as her husband continued his beastly existence,

So Gwendoloena decided to wed – he had given his consent.

One dark night when the horns of the moon were resplendently shining,

All of the lights in the vault of the heavens were brightly illumined,

Clear was the air, more than usual, the freezing and pitiless North wind,

Scouring the skies and expelling the clouds from ethereal regions,

Brought back peace and with dry breath wiped clear every obstruction.   *390*

High on a peak perched Merlin and gazed at the stars in their courses,

Quietly talking to himself under the heavens and saying:

'What means luminous Mars? Is the death of a sovereign portended

By such brilliant light? Will another ascend to that power?

Thus it transpires, I can see, for the king Constantinus has met death,

Conan his nephew assumes now the crown, elevated by spiteful

Fate: he has murdered his uncle the king and then stolen his sceptre.

Now here is Venus on high, whose trajectory slips through the star-signs;

Venus, companion and friend of the sun as it travels the heavens,

Why do you sunder the air with a radiant binary beaming?   400

Does this division portend a divorce from my wife or a parting?

Rays such as this are a sign and a portent of lovers divided.

Has Gwendoloena abandoned her spouse, left me in my absence?

Does she rejoice in embracing another whose arms are her haven?

So I am conquered by him, and another enjoys my beloved;

So I am stripped of my rights while I stubbornly stay in seclusion:

Love that is idle cannot be a winner when love that is active

Stands at the ready to win from its rival the heart of its mistress.

I am not jealous I hope: let her marry with omens propitious,

Let her enjoy her new husband and I will bestow on her blessings,   410

And when the day for the nuptials has dawned then I'll be present

Bearing the present which I had promised before I departed.'

So he did say, then he prowled through the forest and groves of the woodland

And he collected the herds of both stags and of deer in one column,

Goats he collected as well, and he mounted a stag as its rider;

And on the day of the wedding he drove these columns before him,

Rushing to come to the place where the bride was to take her new husband:

After arriving he made all the herds stand still by the doorway,

As, 'Gwendoloena!' he called, 'Gwendoloena! your gifts are awaiting.'

So Gwendoloena arrived in a rush and she laughed at her husband   420

Sitting astride such a beast, yet she saw in astonished amazement

That it obeyed his commands, and that he on his own had collected

Such great numbers of beasts, which he drove from the forest by himself

Just like a shepherd accustomed to leading his sheep to their pasture.

Her bride-groom meanwhile, transfixed by the scene from his window,

Stared at the curious sight of the rider and started to chuckle:

But when the prophet discerned who he was and observed this reaction

All of a sudden he snapped off the horns from the stag he was riding,

Angrily brandishing them he then threw them right at the bride-groom,

Smashing his skull into bits and expelling the life from his body.   430

Spurring his mount he then turned and prepared to retreat to the forest.

Now from around and about the retainers were rushing in pursuit,

Though his escape was assured, so swift was his flight through the country,

Had not a river frustrated his head-long dash to the woodlands:

For as his stag was attempting to leap the impetuous torrent

Merlin was thrown and then fell in the waters so rapidly rushing.

So the retainers encircled the banks and ensnaring the swimmer

Bound him, brought him back as a prisoner home to his sister.

Captured again he was saddened and longed to depart for his much-loved

Forests, and so he assaulted his servants, demanding his freedom,   440

And he refused to be cheerful, food, drink too, he rejected;

Thus did his sadness sadden his sister and move her to sorrow.

Seeing his friend had rejected contentment and spurned his fine banquets,

Rhydderch in pity decided to show him the sights of the city,

Show him the markets and people and novelties sold by the vendors,

Hoping the sight of the bustle and business would raise up his spirits.

While he was making his way from the palace he saw in the entrance

Dressed in some shabby apparel a servant who begged of the passing

People in tremulous voice a few coins to exchange for some new clothes:

Lost in amazement the prophet just laughed at the indigent fellow.   450

Further progressing he noticed a young man holding his new shoes,

Seeking to purchase some patches of leather to mend them when worn-out:

Merlin then laughed once more, and refused to go on through the market

Or be an object of gossip for those he just wanted to observe:

Still he was longing for, looking for, solace in forests secluded,

Striving to retrace footsteps back to forests forbidden.

So the retainers returned home, told of the prophet's amusement,

How he had twice laughed, how he had longed to return to the woodland.

Rhydderch, thus eager to know what occasioned these laughs and their meaning,

Ordered his men to release their unfortunate captive, conceding   460

To him permission to seek his accustomed retreat in the forest,

If he accounted for his smiles – happily Merlin responded:

'That poor man in the doorway dressed as a pauper and begging

Money from bypassers, secretly rich is he (hence my amusement):

Hidden beneath his own feet is a hoard of treasure secreted

Long since – dig up the ground and discover the coins in concealment.

Thence I advanced to the market and saw there a youth with his new shoes

Purchasing patches of leather in order to mend them when worn-out:

Once more laughter arose, since neither the shoes nor the patches

Will be of use to the poor youth now he has drowned in the river,   *470*

Now that his body has floated to shore – it is there for the finding.'

Rhydderch, desiring to prove that the words of the prophet were truthful,

Sent his retainers to search by the river, reporting their findings

If such a body were found drowned: searching the desolate beaches

There they discovered that body and rushed to report to their master.

Meanwhile, Rhydderch removed from the door its custodian beggar,

Dug up the ground and located the hoard that was hidden in secret;

Then he rejoiced at his luck and applauded the wisdom of Merlin.

Having accomplished his part of the bargain, and hating the townsfolk,

Merlin was hoping to leave for the woods when the Queen did detain him,   *480*

Begged him delay his departure 'til winter and frost had abated,

Until the summer returned with its bountiful, succulent produce –

Then he could relish the warmth and the food of the plentiful season;

Scorning both Queen and the cold and still anxious to leave he responded:

'Sister my dear do not strive to detain me – even the storm-filled

Winter cannot stop me, nor the ice-cold blasts of the North wind,

Lashing its hail on the bleating and terrified sheep in the meadows;

Nor does the South wind, stirring relentless the rivers with rainfall,

Ever deter me – still I will seek out the wilds and the green groves:

I am content with but little, and nor am I fearful of frostbite.   490

There in the summer my spirit's delight to recline in the arbors,

And be surrounded by odorous scents of the various flowers.

But I admit I am worried that food will be scarce in the winter,

Therefore, build for me there in the forest a house, with retainers

Who will attend to my needs and prepare all the food I will require

When both the soil lacks plants and the fruits on the branches are lacking.

But, in the first place, build me a house far removed from the others

Which shall have sixty plus ten doors, windows the same in proportion,

So I can study the Sun and its fiery explosions, and Venus

His consort, and the motions of stars as they move in the heavens,   500

Which will inform me of things yet to come for the people and kingdom;

Let there be scribes, too, able to write all my sayings correctly,

And let them strive to record on their pages my verses prophetic.

You, too, dearest of sisters be there, come often to visit,

And with the food and the drink that you bring you will keep me from hunger,'

He said. Then on his fleet feet rushed to his forest beloved.

So did his sister obey him, building the palace commanded

And all the dwellings besides – she complied with whatever he ordered.

Meanwhile, Merlin rejoiced for as long as the trees had their apples,

And as the Sun rose high in the heavens he wandered delighted 510

Where soft zephyrs were whispering gently through rowan plantations;

Then came hoary old winter, which brought harsh storms and tornadoes,

Stripping the branches of fruit and denuding the land of its goodness:

Then as the rain lashed down and the food fell short in the forest,

Hungry and miserable Merlin arrived at his marvellous palace;

Often the Queen met him there, there she would happily serve up

Fine meals – thus was her brother refreshed by the various foodstuffs.

*   *   *

Chapter 6
MERLIN'S PROPHECY

As Merlin wanders about his astronomical–astrological palace in the company of Ganieda, he begins to utter a prophecy about the future fate of the British, describing in elliptical fashion events from his own time up to that of Geoffrey himself. Though the Welsh prophetic tradition upon which Geoffrey drew inspiration was nationalistic – hostility to the invaders, assertions that the Britons would rise again – Geoffrey's main purpose is literary rather than political – for here at last he is able to confirm that this 'wild man' Merlin is one and the same as the prophet of his *History*. Indeed, some of the material presented here is based on passages from Book 11 of his earlier work. At the very of end of the speech, Merlin explicitly states that this was the gist of his prophecy to Vortigern (as related in the *History* – see the Introduction). Despite scattered references that can be deciphered with some confidence, Geoffrey seems less interested in providing a coherent account of historical events than in giving the reader a colourful pastiche of the kind of things the old prophets used to say – the more obscure the metaphor, the more opaque the reference, the better.

The following brief comments are indebted to Basil Clarke's edition (see the Bibliography):

The Cornish boar (line 524) is Arthur, the sons of his line may be the those of his nephew Mordred, the fourth (line 527) is the British king Kareticus, who was besieged at Cirencester by Gormund, king of the Africans ('the sea-wolf', line 528) – Kareticus was driven back across the Severn. Rhydderch's death (line 531) is also predicted by the Welsh Myrddin in the *Cyfoesi*, 'The Dialogue Between Myrddin and his Sister Gwendydd', from the *Red Book of Hergest* (ed. Skene, see the Bibliography). After the Viking destruction of Carlisle (line 544) its bishop (*pastor*) was restored by Henry I ('the Lion'). Caernafon (line 546) is Geoffrey's *Urbs Sigeni* (Roman *Segontium*); Porchester (line 547) and Richborough (line 549) were both busy ports on the South coast. Line 552's Caerleon (*Urbs Legionum*) is on the Usk not the Severn, as Geoffrey surely knew; the 'Bear in the Lamb' may be Augustine of Canterbury. Leicester (line 557) may be a mistake for Chester, where a massacre of monks is attested in the seventh century. The 'first of the Angles to put on the crown of old Brutus' (line 559) is Athelstan (reigned 925–39) – according to Geoffrey's *History*, Britain was founded (and named after), the Trojan exile Brutus. Bishops bearing arms (line 584) happened during the reign of King Stephen (1135–1154). Lines 588–93 presumably refer to the Norman kings following William I's conquest. 'The shade of the helmet' (line 590) is perhaps a Scottish expedition, following in the footsteps of Arthur ('the Boar'). Vortigern's two fighting dragons (lines 594–5) are described in Geoffrey's *History*. The Welsh bard Taliesin (line 598), who will shortly play a prominent part in the poem, is the reputed author of *The Book of Taliesin*, one of the *Four Ancient Books of Wales*. The sixth-century historian Gildas the Wise (line 600) wrote an important account of his age (*De excidio et conquestu Britanniae*, 'On the ruin and conquest of Britain') that was a primary source for later historians such as Bede and Geoffrey himself – the reference to him living in Brittany may be a result of an eleventh-century biography written by a Breton.

Soon he arose from the feast and applauded his sister, her kindness,

Gazed at the stars as he wandered his house and intoned this prediction:

'Mad are the Britons whose pride is excited by riches excessive,   520

Scorning contentment they whip up a frenzy of furious anger

As they engage in both family feuding and communal conflict:

Churches are suffered to fall into ruin, their bishops are banished.

Sons of the line of the Boar that is Cornish are plotting destruction,

Ambushing their own kin, and with impious swords are engaged in

Mutual murder as each, though unlawfully, strives for the kingdom –

Fourth in their line will be one who is crueller and harsher than any:

Him will the sea-wolf conquer in battle, compelling his fast flight

Over the Severn to regions untamed; this wolf will encircle

Cirencester with sparrows, destroying its walls and its houses.   530

Then he will travel to France but will die by the spear of a royal.

When King Rhydderch has died both the Scots and their Cumbrian allies

Will be afflicted by strife, 'til the Cumbrians fall to the long tooth.

Then will the Welsh make war on their neighbours, and Cornwall thereafter –

They are unfettered by laws, and rejoice in both slaughter and bloodshed –

Hateful to God they condemn their own brothers and nephews to conflict.

Warlike Scots will continually transgress over the Humber,

Dealing out death with impunity; death with impunity will strike

He of the horse name, their leader, the fiercest and worst of the Scotsmen;

Then will his heir be expelled from our borders and Scots be required   540

To sheathe bare swords, forced by the strength of our forces ferocious.

Then will Dumbarton collapse and its ruins neglected for ages

Lacking a king to rebuild, 'til the Boar has defeated the Scottish.

Empty will Carlisle stand when deprived of its pastor – revival

Springs from the rod of the Lion that restores the staff to the city.

Then will Caernafon's high turrets lament 'til the Welsh have retreated;

Porchester's walls will collapse in its harbour – restored by the wealthy

Man with the teeth of a fox; and the same demolition is upon

Richborough – it is restored by a Fleming whose vessel is crested;

Fifth in his line will renew and repair Saint David's defences,   550

Likewise, he will return there the shawl that was lost for a lifetime.

Caerleon falls in the lap of the Severn and loses its people –

They will return with the Bear in the Lamb whose arrival is foretold.

Kings of the Saxons will seize all the cities, expelling the natives,

Keeping their homes and their fields while the years drag past for the Britons;

Three times three of their dragons will put on the diadem royal.

Leicester will witness the death of our monks in number two hundred;

Saxons will murder its leader and empty the walls of the city,

Only the first of the Angles to put on the crown of old Brutus

Will have the wit to restore to the city its walls and its people.   560

Murderous tribes will prohibit the sacrament through all the country,

Placing their statues of gods in the houses of God everlasting –

Rome will remove them at last, with the help of a monk, and a holy

Priest will anoint all the churches with water of holiness supreme,

As he restores all the shrines and returns all the priests to their churches,

Dutiful pastors who earn by their piety heavenly favour.

Those same poisonous tribes will confound both the sacred and profane,

Selling their sons and their kindred in far-off lands 'cross the waters.

O vile crime that the freedom of man, God's gift to his children,

Is lost when His men are led captive to market like cattle!   570

O wretch, you who betrayed your lord when your kingdom was new-found,

You will neglect God. Danes will arrive in their ships and will conquer,

Though they will reign for a brief span – home they will go when defeated –

Two are their kings, whom the Serpent shall strike with the sting of its sharp tail

Instead of garlanding their crowns – snakes are unmindful of treaties.

Normans will come in their wood ships, looking both forwards and backwards,

Wearing their iron vests, bearing their sharp swords, killing the Angles

Fiercely they conquer, subduing our kingdoms and overseas nations

Too, 'til a Fury in flight will infect them, dispersing its poison.

Then will depart peace, honour and virtue, the land will be embroiled   580

In war, man will betray man, friendships shall vanish forever,

Husbands despising their wives will take whores and their wives while despising

Husbands will lie with whomever they wish. As the church is dishonoured

So will the bishops then bear arms, follow the army and construct

Turrets and walls on their land once holy and give to the soldiers

What they should give to the needy; ensnared by their riches they pursue

Worldly pursuits, and deny God His due, their duty neglected.

Three will ascend to the throne, they acclaimed by the novelty seekers,

Fourth in that line will be hurt by his powerless piety until,

Clothed like his father, with Boar's teeth, passing the shade of the helmet.   *590*

Of those four just two will succeed to the crown and share it,

This will encourage the Gauls to ferocious attacks on the kingdom;

Having defeated the Irish, the sixth who is pious and prudent

Will then restore our cities and bring back peace to the country.

These things I once predicted to Vortigern, sitting together

Next to the lake where the dragons engaged in their mystical battle.

But you, sister my dear, go home and attend to the dying

King, and then summon my friend Taliesin to come to my palace:

For there is much that I wish to discuss with him – he has just lately

Come from Brittany, where he imbibed all the wisdom of Gildas.'   *600*

*   *   *

Chapter 7
GANIEDA'S GRIEF

At Merlin's bidding, his sister returns to Rhydderch's court but finds the King, her husband, has died. This short but affecting interlude seems to have no precedent in any earlier source – is it fanciful to detect in Ganieda's eloquent lament some of Geoffrey's own longing to renounce worldly things and seek studious retirement?

*   *   *

So Ganieda went home, where she found Taliesin had come back,

But that the King was now dead and his servants enveloped in mourning.

Crying she fell to the floor – though supported by friends she continued

To weep, tearing her hair as she poured out her sorrow in these words:

'Mourn o mourn for my dead king, mourn with me, sisters, remember

Him whose like our age will not see more, nor will the future:

He was a lover of peace, and administered justice with fairness,

Taming the people's ferocity, ending their disputes and violence.

Clergy he treated with kindness, both humble and high were as equals

Under his laws. He was generous, giving a lot but retaining   *610*

83

Little; he did what he could, what was right for his people and proper;

He was the flower of knights and the glory of kings and the pillar

On which his kingdom did rest. Is it true that you lie in your coffin,

Food for the worms, when your bed is prepared with its coverings silken?

Can I believe that the rocks will conceal in their icy embrasures

Your fair limbs, while your body is crumbling to powdery ashes?

Yes I believe – for the fate of us all is the same through the ages

And inescapeable: none can return to their former condition.

Therefore shun the rewards of this transitory world we inhabit,

Even the greatest are caught in the changeable cycle of fortune.   620

Just as the bee first entices with honey then stings the unwary,

So do our secular vanities trick us then hurt us unceasing:

Greatness is fleeting, it flows past us like the stream of a river.

Roses are red and the lilies are blooming, this man is attractive,

This horse graceful, these things are all beautiful – what does it matter?

Let us refer all these worldly concerns to God the Creator.

Happy are those who with pious intentions embrace their redeemer,

Turning their backs on the world and obeying the strictures of their Lord:

Christ the Creator whose reign is eternal bestows on them glory.

Therefore, I will renounce all the comforts of home – its impressive   630

Walls and its high-born nobles and even my children delightful –

And with my brother I'll live in the forest and worship my Lord God

Cheerful in heart but protected by that black cloak on my shoulders.'

Thus did she pay her respects to her husband by speaking so nobly

And by erecting a tomb and inscribing the stone with these verses:

'Rhydderch the Generous – none was more generous than he –

Lies in this modest container, which scarcely retains all his greatness.'

*   *   *

Chapter 8
TALIESIN EXPOUNDS

Alongside his contemporary Myrddin, Taliesin is one of the legendary bardic authors of the *Four Ancient Books of Wales* – though the earliest manuscript of the *Book of Taliesin* itself dates from the fourteenth century it preserves poems of a much earlier period. The first poem in the *Black Book of Carmarthen* is a dialogue between Myrddin and Taliesin, in which they lament the slaughter at the Battle of Arfderydd. This may have been enough of a hint for Geoffrey to bring these two great bards together in his poem.

Merlin asks Taliesin to explain the nature of wind and rain. There follows a learned discourse on natural philosophy as understood by Geoffrey and his educated contemporaries – the different regions of the heavens, earth and sea and their various inhabitants are described: the heavens and its spiritual beings, the various seas and their fish, the notable islands of the earth. Geoffrey's purpose here is partly to ground Merlin's gifts in the natural world, but partly also didactic: presenting scientific knowledge in poetical form had a long history, stretching as far back as Hesiod (*c.* eighth century BC), and it was a pleasant way to impart information to an audience in an age when books were scarce and such knowledge was not generally available. Much of Taliesin's discourse is derived from the writings of the encyclopaedists (see the Introduction) such as Isidore of Seville, who is the main source of the lists of fishes and islands.

Once again, the following comments are indebted to Basil Clarke's edition.

The goddess of wisdom Minerva is invoked (line 641) as the appropriate patroness of scientific knowledge. Bladud (line 730), who is said to have founded the medicinal baths at Bath, is one of the legendary kings of early Britain and features in Geoffrey's *History* as the father of Leir (Shakespeare's King Lear). Thanet (line 732), which lies at the easternmost point of Kent, was a true island in Geoffrey's day. Thule (line 737) is probably Iceland – for the Romans it was the northernmost limit of the world. The Pillars of Hercules (line 745) are the straits of Gibraltar; Hercules travelled to the garden of the Hesperides (line 747) as one of his Labours. According to Isidore, the Gorgades (line 748) are in the Atlantic, while Argyre and Chryse (lines 749–50) and Tiles (line 753) are all said to be in the Indian Ocean. The Fortunate Isle (line 754) is called Avalon in Book 11 of Geoffrey's *History*. Though in Isidore this is a reference to the Canary Islands, Geoffrey significantly alters the context to connect it with the Arthur story (Geoffrey's younger contemporary Gerald of Wales derived the name 'Island of Apples' from the Celtic *Inis Avallon*, which, via the Saxon *Glastingeburi*, gives us modern *Glastonbury*). Here Taliesin provides another bridge between our 'wild man' Merlin and the Merlin of Geoffrey's *History*, by introducing Morgen (line 761) as the ruler of this island who cared for the wounded Arthur after the battle of Camlan – rather as Circe did for Odysseus – a story that seems to be another of Geoffrey's original inventions, as are the names of her sisters (lines 767–8). Like Merlin himself, Morgen has access to specialist scientific knowledge (the medicinal properties of plants, the ability to construct flying wings like Daedalus of old) that seems almost magical: in the hands of later writers she would become the sorceress Morgan Le Fay.

*   *   *

So Taliesin then came to the forest to visit his fellow

Prophet, since Merlin was eager to learn from his friend how the weather

Stirred both the wind and the rain to combine in tempestuous storms-clouds. *640*

Then Taliesin, with help from the goddess Minerva, expounded:

'When the Creator created the four elementary forces

To be the primary cause of creation He made them the basis

Of all the matter created by their own concordant connections:

Star-filled Heaven envelops the rest as a shell does its kernel,

Next comes the sound-filled air through which day is discerned and the night-time,

Then comes the sea which encircles the land and creates with its mighty

Tidal dynamics the winds that are said to be four in their number.

Then the Creator established the earth, fixed firm and unmoving,

This he divided in five – though the zone in the middle is empty   *650*

Thanks to the heat, and the two outside are unsuitably freezing:

Only the two that remain have a pleasant and temperate climate

Where we can live with the birds and the animals flocking together.

Here are the fruits on the branches refreshed by the showers of gentle

Rain from the clouds, which are filled from the rivers like skins full of water,

Helped by the sun in the heavens above – a mysterious process –

Driven by winds to the heights they discharge all their load in a torrent:

Hence we have rain, snow, round hail-stones, too, caused by a chilly

Wet wind driving the clouds to release all their various liquids:

Each of these winds has its birth in a zone and adopts the same nature.   660

Heaven He made in the region beyond where the luminous stars shine

Fit for angelic assemblies to bask in the sweetness of their Lord:

This He adorned with its own sun blazing and stars, and enacted

That all the heavenly bodies have one fixed route for their travels.

Aerial regions that shine with the light of the moon He erected

Under the heavens, where spirits are gathered to join in our sorrows

Or to rejoice in our joy – our prayers are referred up to heaven

By them: they are accustomed to dealing with God for our welfare,

And they convey back to us the compassion of God in our dreaming,

Or through a voice or a sign of some sort that will aid understanding.   670

Under the moon is the place where the spirits of evil are lurking,

Skilled in deception they trick us and tempt us – appearing in bodies

Formed from the air they impregnate our women in unions unholy.

Thus with a three-fold order of spirits the Lord has created

This world – each of them rears and renews the seed of creation.

He has distinguished the sea with its various species of creatures,

So it can bring forth more from itself in abundance forever;

Part of the sea scalds, part chills, temperate parts are sustaining,

But where the sea scalds there is a chasm surrounded by hostile

Tribes, where the zone of the Damned is divided from us by the boiling   *680*

Flow of increasingly hot tides – there go the lawless transgressors

Who have abandoned their God and, perversely impelled by their self-will,

Eagerly rush to accomplish that which is forbidden by Our Lord:

There does the stern judge stand with his scales held in balance impartial,

Dealing to each in accord with their merits their justice deserving.

Chilled is that sea which revolves round its tidy arrangement of beaches,

Formed by itself from the mist as it mingles with radiant Venus:

Arabs relate that this star is the shaper of glittering jewels,

Formed as it passes through Pisces and blazes its light on the oceans:

Gems such as these are a blessing and cure for their wearers.   *690*

Just as with all things, they are distinguished by God the Creator

With their own colour and shape so that we can discern their importance.

It is the third of the seas that confers on us benefits many:

As it encircles our globe it supports all the fishes and produces

Salt in abundance for us, and it carries the ships with our commerce,

Which makes a poor man wealthy by vastly increasing his profits;

And it enriches the neighbouring earth and the birds are supported,

Whom, it is said, are begotten like fish from its plenteous waters,

Though they are moved by a different law to be lords of the heavens

And dominate both the skies and the seas, while the fishes are confined   *700*

Under the waves and cannot be permitted to live in the open:

These the Creator did also divide into species distinctive,

Making both objects of wonder and bringers of health for the infirm.

Let us consider the Barbel, which limits the heat of our passions,

Some say, but which confers on us blindness if eaten too often.

Then there's the Grayling whose scent is so strong that the fishes

Who eat it are revealed by its smell and the river polluted.

Though it has lost all the usual rights of the feminine gender

Still the Murena produces its offspring from seed that is foreign:

Snakes on the shore so beguile the Murenas, seductively hissing,   710

That they successfully copulate, as in the usual manner.

What of the Urchin that, small though it is, can attach to a vessel

Fixing it fast on the sea as if moored to the shore – what a fearsome

Power it has! Swordfish have a sharp beak able to puncture

Timbers of ships, and if caught they make holes and the ship is then flooded;

Sawfish, too, have a sword-like crest that can pierce through the planking.

There is a watery dragon with poisonous fins, and if captured

It will inject its poor captors with poison and injure them badly.

Some say the Ray can inflict on its victims a terrible torpor:

So that one's limbs are as rigid in life as in death by its power.   720

God thus enriched all the seas with such fishes and set in the waters

Fertile, abundant new lands fit for men to develop and flourish.

First and the best of all these is the wonderful island of Britain,

With all its crops and its grain and its woodlands and honey-rich pastures,

Aerial mountains and broad, green meadows and rivers and wellsprings,

Fish, fowl, cattle and wild beasts, fruit on the trees, and jewels,

Valuable metals as well, all supplied by ingenious Nature.

Worthy of note, our salubrious hot springs succour the needy,

Soothing their sickness in pleasantly warming and curative waters;

Bladud established these baths which are named for his consort Alaron: *730*

They are especially useful in curing diseases of women.

Next to our island lies Thanet, abounding in valued resources,

Though it is lacking in poisonous snakes, hence if earth from this island

Added to wine is imbibed it removes all the dangerous poison.

Our sea separates us from the thirty-three islands of Orkney,

Twenty of which are not farmed, but the others are tilled by their people.

Thule is described as the 'Furthest' since that is the place where the summer

Sun stands still and does not move or illuminate further:

Night is perpetual there, and the cold air freezes the ocean,

Making a ship's navigation impossible via the ice-sea. *740*

Famously fertile is Ireland, surpassing in beauty all others,

Except of course our own – it has few birds, bees it is lacking,

Snakes are unable to live on its soil, and if moved to another

Place both its rocks and its earth will destroy all the bees and the serpents.

Gades is next to the Pillars of Hercules – there it produces

Trees from which gum is distilled: glass smeared with it changes to jewels.

There is a dragon, they say, of Hesperides guarding the golden

Apples that grow on the trees. It is said that the female Gorgades,

Hairy as goats, run faster than hares. Both the islands of Argyre

And that of Chryse are rich in both silver and gold; while in Ceylon   *750*

Two crops bloom in the doubled-up seasons of spring and of summer,

And its inhabitants gratefully gather its grapes and its gem-stones;

Tiles produces its fruits and its flowers in spring everlasting.

That which is known as the Island of Apples is Fortunate also,

So-called because it brings forth harvests in fields where no ploughmen

Labour, but rather its crops grow just by the action of Nature:

Grapes it abounds in and apples are born from the grass of its woodlands,

Everything grows in abundance and men live there for a hundred

Years or occasionally more. Nine sisters benignly empowered

Rule there over all those who arrive at that island from our lands.   *760*

First and most skilled of them all, both in healing and beauty, is Morgen,

Who has a knowledge of plants, both their uses and curative powers;

Such is her skill that she knows how to change her own shape, and on wondrous

Wings she can fly just as Daedalus flew, and she flies past the cities,

As is her wont, or she glides through the air then alights on your shoreline;

And she imparted her knowledge of science and maths to her sisters,

Moronoe, Mazoe, Gliten, Glitonea, Gliton,

Tryronoe, and that Thiten most famous for playing her lyre.

Thither we carried poor Arthur when grievously wounded at Camlan:

Steering our ship was Barinthus, who knew both the tides and the heavens,   *770*

So he could guide us in safety to Morgen, who welcomed us warmly.

Arthur was laid in her chamber on her own bed with its golden

Coverings: there she did lay her own hands on his wounds and did ponder

Long, then at last she declared his wounds could be healed if he stayed there

And he agreed to be treated by her: so we gladly accepted,

Leaving the king in her care and departing on favourable currents.'

*   *   *

Chapter 9
THE KINGS OF BRITAIN

Prompted by Taliesin's mention of Arthur, Merlin briefly prophesies the future calamities that the British will suffer under Saxon overlordship now that Arthur has gone. Then he is led to recollect the events of recent history (line 806 onwards), once again reinforcing the identity of this Merlin with the Merlin of Geoffrey's *History*. Conan and Cadwalader (796–7) are the two kings in Welsh tradition who are to restore the island to the British. In Geoffrey's *History*, Conan is Conan Meriadoc, founder of Brittany; while Cadwalader is the last king of the Britons, who – at the end of Book 11 – is called away by an angelic voice that tells him the Britains are no longer to rule in Britain, 'until the time had come which Merlin had prophesied to Arthur'. According to the *History*, the Trojan exile Brutus (800) was the first king of the Britons.

The historical reminiscence begins with the murder of Constans by Vortigern, who seized the kingdom but only held onto it with the help of the treacherous Anglo-Saxons, led by brothers Hengist and Horsa. Vortigern is betrayed and flees – in the *History*, Merlin makes his first appearance as Vortigern is in hiding (see the Introduction) – while his son Vortimer drives out the invaders, but to no avail: his stepmother Rowena (Geoffrey calls her *Renua*), who is also Hengist's sister, poisons him and the Saxons return. Constans' two younger brothers, Aurelius Ambrosius and Uther, come back from exile in Brittany. Ambrosius kills Vortigern and takes his crown, then defeats the invaders. After a short reign (Geoffrey specifies *lustra quaterna*, which could be sixteen but is more likely to be four years) he is succeeded by Uther, who continues to fight the Angles and Saxons. Uther fathers Arthur, who, with the aid of the Breton King Hoel, drives out the Angles and then conquers all the lands surrounding Britain: in Book 9 of the *History* he fights in single combat with Frollo (line 883), the Roman governor of France. But Arthur is betrayed by his nephew Mordred and falls at the battle of Camlan. Mordred's sons vie for the kingdom, but his nephew Constantine takes the crown, only to be betrayed by the Conan whom Merlin has mentioned earlier (Chapter 5, lines 395–6) – Aurelius Conanus, not to be confused with the Conan Meriadoc of line 796.

*　　*　　*

Merlin replied to his friend: 'O dearest companion, what trouble

Since has afflicted our kingdom now that the oath has been broken:

Nobles are gripped by misfortune and tear at each other's own vitals,

Riches abandoned, prosperity fled, and all else in commotion,   *780*

Cities are emptied of people as Saxons with fearsome equipment

Batter their walls and return so savage to conquer we Britons,

Temples of God violated and His laws, too, as we suffer

Ruin arising from our own folly – a punishment divine ...'

Merlin had not yet completed his speech when his friend interrupted:

'Hence we must summon the king to return in a rapidly sailing

Vessel, assuming he's well, to defend with his customary vigour

Our homes, driving the enemy back and restoring our freedom.'

'Not so,' Merlin replied, 'will that tribe be compelled to relinquish

All of the lands it has stolen from us and seized in its talons;   790

First it will strangle our kingdom, people and cities with fearsome

Force and subdue us for many a year, though resisted by three men

Of our race who will slaughter the foe till at last they are conquered;

For it is willed by the highest of judges that Britain shall languish

Under that yoke and the British deprived of a leader for ages,

Until the time when from Brittany comes in a chariot Conan

And that Cadwalader, venerable chief of the Welsh, who will unite

Clans of the Cornish, the Scots and the Welsh, with the Bretons as allies,

Thus to restore to the natives the crown that was lost by removing

The dread foe and reviving the glories of the empire of Brutus: 800

Britons will rule in their cities once more and administer just laws;

Kings of the Britons will once more conquer the kingdoms of others.'

Said Taliesin: 'But none who are now in the land of the living

Will be alive to enjoy it – not you even, I suppose,

Who has seen more of the cruelty of war than can rightly be endured.'

Merlin replied, 'It is so – I have lived long, witnessed a great deal:

Wars of our own so destructive, barbarian tribes and their chaos.

And I recall the betrayal of Constans, the flight of his brothers

Uther and youthful Ambrosius, forced into flight from their homeland;

So there was war in the kingdom, then lacking a leader to save it: *810*

Vortigern, consul of Gwent, led his armies to battle and slaughter,

Killing the innocent, bringing destruction wherever he travelled,

Finally seizing the crown in a sudden attack he then murdered

Most of the nobles and brought to its knees all the land as his fiefdom.

But all the friends of the brothers in exile then began disputing

Vortigern's claim, and they burnt all his cities, disturbing his kingdom

And not permitting the miserable king to have peace or contentment.

Hence their rebellion compelled him to summon assistance from afar:

Soon he was joined by some squadrons of foreigners, warriors fearsome,

Then came the Saxons in curved ships, bringing their helmeted soldiers;   *820*

Bold were their leaders, called Hengist and Horsa, whose wicked betrayal

Ruined the land and its cities and people: they claimed they were loyal,

But when they saw that the natives were fighting in mutual conflict,

And just how easy it was to subdue both the king and his kingdom,

They broke faith and they turned on the people, betraying the nobles,

Whom they had summoned to parlay but faithlessly murdered them instead;

Vortigern fled through the snow to the mountains (this fate I had foretold)

Just as the Saxons set fire to the homes of the people and forced them to submit.

Vortimer, son of the king, took the crown which his father abandoned,

He was proclaimed our new leader and fought with the foe in engagements *830*

Many and drove them to Thanet, the place where their vessels were lying –

Horsa was killed while retreating and hordes of the enemy slaughtered –

There he beseiged them by land and by sea, but the Saxons with violent

Force broke through with their ships and returned to their home in a hurry.

So with these triumphs was Vortimer hailed by the world as a ruler

Worthy of honour who ruled his new kingdom with justice and mildness.

But then Rowena the sister of Hengist was tortured by hatred,

She meditated the murder of her own dutiful step-son:

Mixing a poison she gave it to him and he drank it with gusto,

And so he died. Then she summoned her brother to sail with his army   840

Back to our land, and to bring with him soldiers sufficient to conquer:

This was accomplished and Hengist grew fat on the spoils he had stolen

As he was putting our homes to the torch and despoiling the country.

Now at this time was Ambrosius staying with Uther his brother

Over in Brittany: Budic the King of the Bretons was their host;

There they did learn all the war-like arts and were tested in battle,

There they had gathered from various regions an army to invade

Britain and drive out the Saxons who clung to our island like leeches.

So to the winds and the tides they committed their ships and alighted

On our shores, and they followed the footsteps of Vortigern throughout   850

Wales till they found his tower and burnt it with Vortigern inside.

Then they advanced on the Angles with weapons unsheathed and defeated

Them in a series of battles, but sometimes were beaten in their turn.

Finally, victory came to our side when in desperate combat

Hengist was killed by the will of our Lord and Ambrosius triumphed –

So he was crowned as our king and was praised by the people and clergy.

Mildly he ruled and with justice, but the days of his reign were soon over:

He was betrayed by a doctor and died by imbibing a poison.

Uther succeeded his brother but reigned just as peace proved elusive,

For the perfidious tribes now returned, as they threatened so often,   *860*

Landing their forces and ravaging all in their usual manner;

Uther resisted them bravely and forced them to flee to their homeland;

Peace he restored for a while and he sired then a son who was destined

For such a marvellous fame as to outshine all who would follow:

Arthur would reign when his father had died, but with grief and hard labour,

Since he would fight in innumerable battles and bloody engagements,

For, while his father was dying, the Angles invaded the country –

All of the region across from the Humber fell prey to their weapons.

Hampered by youth and inexpert in battle the boy was unable

To curb such great hordes; so consulting the clergy and people   *870*

He then asked Hoel, who was king of the Bretons, to give his assistance –

Hoel was connected by kin and by love to his friend the young Arthur,

Each was obliged by this friendship to come to the aid of the other –

Therefore Hoel did assemble his fleet and arrived with his armies,

Joining with Arthur he struck at the enemy, often attacking,

Frequently slaughtering them; this alliance gave power to Arthur

Which he employed in attacking and driving the foe to their homeland.

Victory gained, he then ruled in the kingdom with sense and with justice.

After these wars he amended his strategy, beating the war-like

Irish and Scots, and then using his forces to conquer the nations   880

Farther away: the Norwegians who live far over the ocean,

Danes, too, dreaded the sight of his fleet – both fell to his armies.

Frollo the legate of Rome he then killed and so conquered the people

Of France. Since they had schemed to remove him from power in battle

Even the Romans were beaten by Arthur, who killed their own leader,

Lucius Hiberius, who was ordered by Emperor Leo

And by the Senate of Rome to retrieve all the lands they had ceded.

But back in Britain the infamous Mordred, a treacherous regent,

Seized for his own both the crown and the Queen, with whose love he was trifling;

Arthur had trusted his lands and his Queen to perfidious Mordred,   890

So when he heard that this man had betrayed him with malice aforethought

He was compelled to return to this country, deferring his campaigns.

Landing with thousands of troops he attacked and defeated his nephew

Mordred, who fled from the country then gathered an army of Saxons:

So he continued the war – but the Saxons then broke their allegiance,

First they betrayed and then murdered their leader, whose trust had been misplaced.

Such was the slaughter of men on that field and the mourning of mothers

Whose sons fell there, killed in that blood-soaked, terrible battle!

There on the same field, Arthur our King fell mortally wounded;

Hence he was sent, as related by you, to the Isle of the maidens.   900

Mordred had two sons, each of whom fought for the right to be ruler,

Striving in battle, refusing to yield as they slaughtered their kinsmen;

Then did Constantine, nephew of Arthur, make war on the duo,

Violently mangling their people and brutally killing the brothers,

So he could take up the crown of the king and give laws to the nation.

But he was not to have peace: for his kinsman Conan revolted,

Started calamitous war and accomplished the death of his rival;

Then he despoiled all the wealth of this country which feebly he now rules.'

*   *   *

Chapter 10
THE HEALING WATERS

At last Merlin is freed from his madness thanks to the curative waters of a new spring that has suddenly begun to flow. As a result he is deprived of the ecstatic out-of-body experience (line 928) that gave him the ability to make prophecies. Merlin professes relief that the madness has gone, since it had allowed him to know the hidden secrets of the universe – the flights of birds, motions of the stars, swimming of the fishes and the like – and this was just too distressing. Such knowledge, apparently, is too much of a burden for a mere mortal. Curiously, then, after thanking God for his deliverance Merlin immediately turns to Taliesin and requests more of the same! Clearly his thirst for learning remains unquenched.

Healing springs are a common theme in Celtic mythology and are often associated with an oracle or seer – Nikolai Tolstoy (*The Quest for Merlin*) even traces a link between Merlin and Hartfell Spa, a chalybeate (iron-rich) spring on the slopes of Hart Fell, near Moffat in southern Scotland. The healing power of water thus becomes a natural subject for discussion, and Taliesin once more begins a learned discourse. His list follows closely the one in Isidore of Seville's encyclopaedia, though by no means all of the rivers, lakes and springs mentioned in Isidore were known for their medicinal effects.

While he was saying these things, some retainers appeared in a hurry,

Eager to tell him they'd found a new spring at the foot of the mountains 910

Gushing with waters so pure and refreshing, which flowed down the valley

Into the pastures and swirled into streams with murmuring gurgles.

So Taliesin and Merlin arose and then rushed to the site of the fountain;

Merlin there sat on the grass and admired the pellucid outpouring

Waters and wondered just how they could spring from the earth in this manner.

Then he was captured by thirst and so bending he drank from the river,

Washing his brow at the same time: thus as the liquid was coursing

Through all his innards it gave him relief from the heat of his organs,

Calming both body and mind, so he came to his senses and banished

Madness entirely as feeling revived and his former existence, 920

Healthy and sane, was restored to him then and his reason recaptured.

So he gave praise to the Lord as he lifted his eyes to the heavens,

And with a voice that was full of devotion he gratefully declaimed,

'O King – You who created the stars and decided their motions,

You who ensures both the sea and the earth are productive and useful,

Fertile, abundant in seed and in crops for the pleasure of mankind,

You who restored both my sense and my sanity, banishing error –

Fleet like a spirit was I and removed from myself as I beheld

All of the deeds of the world and of men and predicted the future;

And I discerned all the secrets of nature – the birds and their flying, 930

Stars and their wandering movements, and fish as they glide through the waters –

Though it distressed me to know how the universe worked in this manner,

So did that knowledge deprive me of natural human contentment;

Now I am me once again, and I seem to be moved by that former

Vigorous motion of spirit that bolsters the strength in my muscles.

I am beholden to You, therefore, O greatest of fathers,

Wholly deserving this praise from a heart that is filled with your praises,

Joy and libations I offer to You everlastingly joyful;

Doubly I gained from the generous gift of your hand when it offered,

Fresh from the green earth, water to drink that restored me my senses;   *940*

Drinking the waters has given my mind all the health it was lacking.

But, my beloved companion, from whence has this power arisen

That such a new spring flows whose waters restored me to myself?'

So Taliesin replied: 'The enriching director of all things,

Having distinguished the different species of streams, in addition

Added to each its own power to help in the cure of the needy:

Hence the medicinal springs, lakes, rivers all over our planet.

Swift the salubrious waters of Tiber do flow through the Roman

City, where wounds (it is said) are repaired by its sure medication;

Also in Italy, Cicero's Spring mends eyes that are damaged.   *950*

In Ethiopia there is a pool, some say, where the water

Glistens like oil when applied to one's face; while the African Zema

Furnishes liquid that gives to one's voice a melodious sweetness.

Those who have drunk from the Lake of Clitorius find it is irksome

To drink wine; they grow sluggish who drink from the fountain of Chios.

Grecian Boeotia has two springs – one makes the drinker remember,

One makes them forget; a lake in the same place causes excessive

Fury and lust, while the Cyzicus Spring puts a stop to all loving;

But in Campania the rivers change women from sterile to fertile;

Those same rivers, they say, can abolish the rage of their menfolk.   960

The Ethiopian spring with a ruddy appearance produces

Madness if drunk; but the spring of Leinus prevents an abortion;

Sicily boasts two springs – if they drink from one or the other

Girls are made barren or, happily, suddenly find they are fertile.

Drinking from one of a pair of Thessalian rivers will render

White sheep black, but the other restores their original colour:

Drinking from both will ensure that the sheep have a coat that is mottled.

Huge are the oxen Clitumnus in Umbria sometimes produces;

Horses have hooves made hard by the crossing of marshy Reatine.

People who swim do not sink in the Asphalt Lake of Judaea,   970

But if you try you will sink to the bottom of Indian Syden,

Nothing can sink in the Lake of Aloe, not even a lead weight –

Just as the stones in the Marside Spring stay afloat on its surface.

Styx in Arcadia springs from a rock and its waters are deadly;

Over a number of days does the Spring Idumaean change colour:

First it is dirty, then green in succession, then bloody, then limpid,

And for a quarter of each year each of the colours is maintained.

Three times daily the Troglodyte lake flows with water quite bitter,

Three times daily with water that's sweet to the taste and quite pleasant.

Torches if dipped in the fountain of Epirus blaze into brightness,   *980*

So it is said, but it also extinguishes light from those torches.

The Garamantes have springs that are freezing by day but are boiling

At night – any approach is denied by the heat and the coldness.

Many such springs have a dangerous heat, which is gained as they flow through

Sulphur or alum, whose powers of warming are useful in treatment.

God has enriched all the waters with these and additional virtues,

So that the sick can be cured in a trice, while revealing the goodness

Of the Creator, preeminent in and above all of Nature.

Here are salubrious waters whose curative strength is impressive,

So I suppose and consider your marvellous cure is the result   *990*

Of their erupting so freshly from dark subterranean caverns,

Where they had travelled like many such streams, 'til their journey was broken

Perhaps by rocks or some earth or another collapsing obstruction,

Forcing the water to make a diversion, and hence it erupted

Out of the ground and created this spring, which like many such rivers

Seeks to return once more to its underground course through the caverns.'

*   *   *

Chapter 11
MERLIN AND THE BIRDS

Despite being cured of his madness, Merlin chooses not to return to 'normal' life, even when asked to resume his kingship – remember he was introduced at the beginning of the poem as King of the Demetae – but opts instead to continue his academic pursuits in his beloved Caledonian forest. The curious sight of cranes flying overhead in a letter-shaped formation elicits another learned disquisition, once more derived from Isidore. But this time it is Merlin's turn to hold forth: now that he is sane again, here is an opportunity to prove that he is Taliesin's equal as a natural philosopher – his description of birds mirrors Taliesin's earlier list of fishes (Chapter 8). This is the last list of 'wonders of nature' that help us to understand Merlin's apparently supernatural powers as a part of the natural order: his divinatory gifts seem less magical in a world that contains such things as singing swans and combustible phoenixes. (The Memnon of line 1083 was an Ethiopian king killed by Achilles during the Trojan War.)

By now Merlin has come a long way from the 'wild man of the woods' of the poem's earlier chapters. And though he has also been stripped of his supernatural powers of prophecy, Geoffrey has now transformed him into something more congenial: a man of learning.

*   *   *

While they discoursed on this subject, a rumour was widely dispersing

That in the depths of the woods Caledonian water was rising

Fresh from the ground which had cured all the ills of a man who had drunk it,

Who for a long time suffered from madness and lived like a wild beast.　　　1000

Soon came the chieftains and leaders to see and congratulate Merlin

On his remarkable cure, and they told him the state of his country

And they implored him to take up the sceptre again and to govern

Once more his people as once he had governed with fairness and justice.

Merlin responded, 'My young friends, old age spurns such a demand:

Time has so weakened my limbs that I struggle to walk through the pastures;

More than my fair share I have enjoyed – all those days to be savoured,

All that abundance of riches that smiled on my fortunate person.

There in the forest an oak stands tall – in its prime it was robust,

Now it is rotted by age and its sap is unable to sustain　　　1010

It – I have watched it develop from just one acorn I observed

Falling by chance to the ground, as a woodpecker perched in the branches;

All of its stages I viewed as it grew with spontaneous vigour,

I was in awe of that spot and committed the place to my memory.

As you can see I have lived long, age is to me now a burden,

So I will reign no more. Caledonian greenery delights

Me more than jewels from India, gold from the banks of the Tagus,

Corn from Sicilian fields, or the grapes on the vines of sweet Methis;

More than the highest of towers, or cities encircled by bastions,

Or clothes scented with Tyrian perfume: none can divert 1020

Me from my dear Caledonian wood, where I live in contentment

Dining on fruits and on herbs, where my flesh will be cleansed by a pious

Fast, so that I will rejoice in a life everlastingly endless.'

As he was speaking the chieftains discerned in the emptiness above

Cranes that were flying in curved lines forming the shape of a letter;

Wondering at this they demanded that Merlin explain this formation.

So he replied to them saying, 'The birds, just as all of creation,

Have been assigned their own nature uniquely by God the designer:

This I have learned as the long days passed while I lived in the forest.

Such is the nature of cranes as they roam in a flock through the heavens 1030

That they are frequently formed into shapes of one kind or another,

Warned by the cries of their leader to keep their formation unbroken;

But when his voice has grown hoarse and is failing he yields to another;

During the night they are watchful – their sentinel holds in his talons

A stone, thwarting the onset of sleep – when intruders are noticed

All are aroused by the noise; all their feathers are darkened by old age.

Such is the vision of Eagles (whose name is derived from its keenness),

That it is said they can stare at the sun and their eyes are not damaged;

Chicks are suspended in its rays lest, by avoiding its brightness,

One is revealed as a weakling; as high as a mountain they hover 1040

Over the water and spy out prey in the depths of the ocean:

All of a sudden they dive and the fate of the fish is decided.

Vultures conceive and give birth to their young, it is wondrous to relate,

Though they are scornful of sex and the seed of their husband is missing;

Flying like eagles they soar in the heavens and sniff out cadavers

Far out to sea, which they quickly approach and then gorge on the corpses

Eagerly; these birds live for a century, such is their vigour.

Storks with their chattering beaks bring the news of the onset of springtime,

Such is their love for their offspring, some say, that they pluck from their own breasts

Feathers; avoiding the storms of the winter they fly off to Asia   1050

Guided, some say, by a crow; at the end of their lives they are nourished

By their own chicks, who were fed in their turn when they needed protection.

Swans, who are dear to all sailors, will sing as they die a delightful

Song that is sweeter than all of the songs of their winged companions;

In Hyperborean lands, it is said, they will sing to a lyre,

Being attracted to shore by the sound if by chance they should hear it.

Ostriches bury their eggs in the dirt then abandon their offspring,

So they are hatched by the rays of the sun not the care of their mother.

Herons retreat to the clouds when a dangerous storm is impending;

Thus does their flight give a warning to sailors that rain is approaching.   1060

But in the land of the Arabs the Phoenix uniquely refreshes

Its own body, a heavenly gift; when enfeebled by old age,

In a location that's warmed by the sun, it amasses a massive

Heap made from spices – this funeral pyre it ignites with a rapid

Flapping of wings, then it sits on the top, is entirely cremated,

Thence from the ashes it rises anew, so survives through the ages.

The Cinnamolgus constructs out of cinnamon nests in the tall oaks,

Which are removed by the arrows of men and then sold in the market.

Pools by the sea are frequented by Halcyons, birds that in winter

Build nests – while they are nesting the sea stays calm for a whole week,   *1070*

Winds cease, storms are restrained, so the bird is relaxed and unruffled.

Parrots can mimic the sound of a human, if no one is watching,

So it is thought, and combine their hello-ing and greeting with joking.

Pelicans kill their own nestlings and mourn in confusion for three days,

Then with their beaks they will peck their own bodies, releasing in rivers

Blood from their veins which is dropped on the chicks – so restoring their being.

Diomed birds, it is said, with their cries so lamentably mournful,

Warn of the sudden decease of a king or a kingdom in peril;

But when approached by a stranger they know if he's Greek or if foreign:

Greeks they applaud with their wings and approach with a flattering chirping;   *1080*

Others like foe are attacked with a horrible flapping and shrieking.

Memnonid birds each fifth year make a migration to visit

Troy and the tomb where their leader is laid and they mourn for their Memnon.

One of the marvellous feathers the wondrous Hercynian birds bear

Shines like a lamp in the darkness and lights up the way for the bearer.

Woodpeckers pluck from the trees where they nest all the nails and the wedges

That no other could move, while the forest resounds with their knocking.'

Chapter 12
MAELDIN THE MAD

Enter a new madman, Maeldin, a companion of Merlin's youth who was driven insane when he accidentally ate poisoned apples intended for Merlin by a malicious former lover. (The Arwystli of line 1098 is part of the Welsh district of Powys.) Despite similarities of name with the Irish *Mael Duin* and Welsh *Maelgwn Gywnedd*, the story of Maeldin seems to be another of Geoffrey's highly original inventions. Maeldin's sudden appearance allows us an opportunity to see another side of Merlin – his compassion. Cured by the spring waters, Maeldin is invited by Merlin to stay with him and serve God. Taliesin volunteers to stay, too, and so Merlin's pious and scholarly community is formed. At a busy time in his own life when plans were afoot for him to become a bishop, Geoffrey may have indulged himself in this pleasant fantasy of Merlin's woodland university.

*　　*　　*

Just as he finished a madman suddenly made an appearance –

Brought to their notice by Fortune perhaps? – who then filled up the forest

With such a noise like a wild boar, raging and spluttering madly.　　*1090*

Quickly they seized him, compelled him to sit, as they hoped that by speaking

113

This madman would supply them with laughter and jokes for their pleasure.

Merlin examined the man with attention then groaned in deep sorrow

As he recalled who he was, and so spoke: 'This man is much altered

Now from the time when we both were enjoying the flower of our youth;

He was a noble and virtuous soldier of lineage royal,

One of my fellows, and richly endowed with such friends I was happy.

One day, while we were roaming the towering peaks of Arwystli,

Under the broadening boughs of an oak tree heavenwards straining

We saw flowing a spring that was girded by emerald grasses;   *1100*

Sweet was its water and we were all thirsty and parched, so we sat there

Eagerly quaffing the cool, clear stream – then we noticed some fragrant

Apples that lay on the delicate grass by the side of the river:

He who had first caught sight of them laughed at this welcome refreshment,

Gave them to me to dispense as a gift to my fellows, but empty

Handed was I when I'd finished my giving – the apples had run out.

So all my friends laughed, calling me generous, greedily chewing,

Chomping the fruit while complaining the apples were small and too scanty.

Suddenly mad they became – the unfortunate, miserable fellows –

Reason had fled and like mad dogs each of them bit one another,   *1110*

Scratching and barking and drooling and losing their minds in the process;

Finally they left, filling the air with their pitiful wolf-like

Howling; I guessed that the apples were destined for me not my comrades –

Later I learned this was true: a revengeful old lover, whose passion

I had once sated for many a year, but then spurned and rejected

Her and her sexual favours, determined to hurt me in any

Way that she could: when alternative schemes had not come to fruition,

She smeared apples with poison, positioned them them under the oak tree

Where I would pass by, hoping to do me harm by these foul means,

If I should eat of the apples discovered by chance on the greensward;   1120

Luckily Fortune preserved me from hurt, though my friends had to suffer.

Now as for this man, let him imbibe these salubrious waters,

Thence to regain, if he's able, his health and be freed from his madness;

Then for the rest of his days he can stay here with me in the forest,

Doing the work of the Lord.' So the madman drank from the water,

And he was cured and recovered from madness and knew all his fellows.

Merlin then spoke to him, saying, 'The service of God is your duty

Now you can see you are yourself once more, you who had wandered

Shamelessly wild in the woods like a beast; do not flee from the bushes,

Nor from the green groves cherished in madness, but stay, my companion,   1130

Stay here with me and the days that were stolen from you by that mighty

Madness the work of the Lord shall restore to you. Share my possessions,

That which is mine shall be yours, we shall prosper and thrive in the forest.'

Maeldin, for that was his name, then replied, 'O venerable father,

This is an offer I cannot refuse – I will live here with gladness,

Worshipping God in the forest with you, just as long as my trembling

Limbs and my mind are inspired I will follow your lead as my master.'

Then Taliesin responded, 'A third I will add to your party:

Long has the secular world and its vanities robbed my contentment;

Now with your leadership I will have time to discover my true self. 1140

But, my lords, you must leave and accord to your cities protection;

You should no longer disturb our peaceful existence with such talk:

Merlin is tired of your praise.' So the chieftains returned to their cities.

*   *   *

Chapter 13
GANIEDA THE PROPHETESS

To the three men a fourth person is now joined – Ganieda, Merlin's sister. It would be centuries before women could attend actual universities, but here in Merlin's harmonious woodland retreat Ganieda is accorded equal status. Not only that, she inherits her brother's prophetic powers and is the only other person in the poem to utter a prophecy, this one specifically concerned with the events of Geoffrey's own time.

Much of Stephen's reign (1135–1154) was marked by civil war between him and the daughter of Henry I, the Empress Matilda. Ganieda's reference to Oxford (line 1151) probably refers to the Church Council held there in 1139, when two bishops were arrested by King Stephen's men – the Bishop of Ely fled to the castle of Bishop Roger of Devizes, who was then forced to open it (lines 1153–4). Lincoln (line 1155) was beseiged by Stephen in 1141, but when Randolf of Chester managed to escape and summon the help of Matilda's half-brother, the Welsh leader Robert of Gloucester, Stephen was captured and briefly imprisoned at Bristol. In the same year Winchester saw a battle between the two Matildas ('the two moons', line 1160) – Empress Matilda and Stephen's wife, Queen Matilda, whose general William d'Ypres routed the queen's enemies: the Empress was rescued from disaster by a Breton count, Geoffroi of Penthièvre ('the Brittany boar', line 1168). The battle under the mound of Urien (line 1170) may be the Battle of Coleshill, Flintshire, in 1150 – King Coel ('Old King Cole') was one of the legendary early kings of Britain, according to Geoffrey's *History*. Deira (line 1172) was a kingdom of northern Britain. The Normans (line 1180) are possibly the troops belonging to Queen Matilda, or those of her son Henry who, following the Treaty of Wallingford in which Stephen recognised him as his successor, would become King Henry II in 1154.

So the story concludes with a passing of the prophetic torch. Unlike later authors, who would have the hapless wizard ensnared by wicked sorceresses and imprisoned in an enchanted tomb (or cave, or rock, etc.), when kindly Geoffrey signs off he leaves his friend Merlin to enjoy retirement in peace.

*   *   *

Now Ganieda, the sister of Merlin, remained with the three men,

Having adopted their manner of life – she had longed for retirement

After the death of her husband the king; though once ruler of nations

Now she found nothing more sweet than to live in the woods with her brother.

Sometimes she was inspired by her spirit to sing of the future:

Once, as she stood in the hall of her brother and gazed at the palace

Windows that gleamed in the sunlight, she uttered ambiguous phrases   *1150*

From an ambiguous heart: 'I see Oxford surrounded by soldiers,

Bishops and men of the cloth chained, such is the will of the Council:

Then is the Shepherd surprised in the highest of towering turrets,

Forced to unlock his own castle he suffers distress for no purpose.

Lincoln beseiged, I can see, by the fiercest of soldiers and two men

Shut in its walls – one escapes and returns with the chief of a fearsome

People, then conquers the army of savages, seizing their leader:

O it is wrong that the sun is thus captured by stars: though not constrained

Either by force or by war, still they must fade as it rises.

Two moons rise in the air near to Winchester, two are the lions 1160

Fighting ferociously there; one man at two others is gazing,

Two are espied by another, preparing for war they are ready:

Rising they fight with the fourth but they fail to prevail in the bitter

Battle, for he stands firm with his shield and repels all their missiles;

Now as the victor he speedily tramples his triple opponents:

Two are impelled to return to the cold of the North, while the other

Asks and is granted a pardon; the stars therefore are thus scattered

Over the whole of the field. But the Brittany boar, girt with ancestral

Oak, has now rescued the full moon, whirling his swords as protection.

Underneath Urien's mound I can see two stars set to fighting 1170

Savagely like wild beasts – in the reign of great Coel there had gathered

Men from both Deira and Gwent – as the sweat from the soldiers is dripping

So is the blood on the ground while the foreign invaders are wounded.

Having collided with others a star now falls into shadow,

Hiding its light though the light is restored. Now famine has fallen

Hard on the people, their bellies are pinched and their limbs are quite weakened:

Coming from Wales it then spread to the furthermost parts of the kingdom,

Forcing the miserable people to leave home, crossing the ocean.

Calves once accustomed to drink Scotch milk from the cows that are dying

In the disaster have fled. Leave, Normans! Your arms are not welcome   1180

Here in our land, nor your violent soldiers: your gullet is sated,

Nothing is left to be eaten that Nature once bountiful brought forth.

O Christ, succour your people, restrain those furious lions,

Stop all their wars and so give to our kingdom some peace and contentment.'

She did not end with this plea – her companions still listened in wonder;

Merlin her brother applauded her speech and with words of fond friendship

Said, 'Is it you whom the spirit has chosen to sing of the future,

My dear sister, and closed both my mouth and the book of the prophet?

Let it be given to you, therefore, and rejoice in its power:

Under my auspices truthfully speak what your spirit discloses.'   1190

*   *   *

Now we have brought our song to completion – so Britons, the laurel

Wreath must be given to Geoffrey of Monmouth, the very same Geoffrey

Who had once sung of your wars and the wars of your kings, and he published

Them in that eminent book which is known as the *Deeds of the Britons*.

*   *   *

INDEX OF NAMES

References are to line numbers in the poem

In Robert de Boron's thirteenth-century poem *Merlin*, the wizard is depicted dictating his prophecies to his master, Blaise.

ALSO PUBLISHED BY AMBERLEY

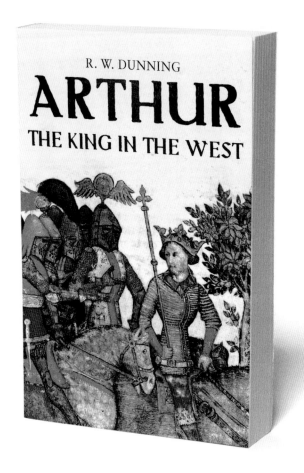

ARTHUR – THE KING IN THE WEST

978-1-84868-242-9

235 x 165 mm | paperback | 176 pages

£12.99

For more information visit:
www.amberleybooks.com

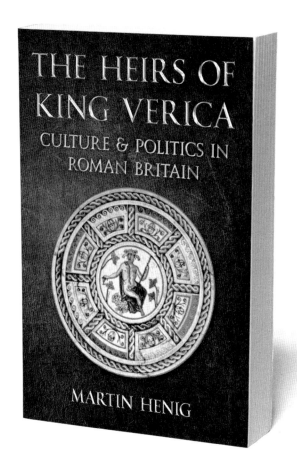

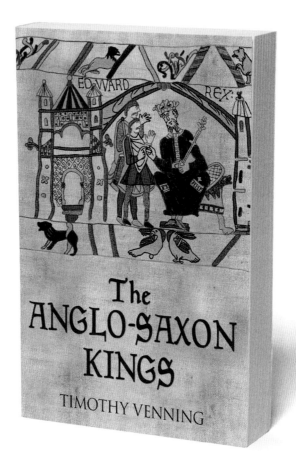